Seattle Travel Guide 2015

Don't Miss Travel Guides

Author: Julie Goodyear

Foreword

FREE BONUS - By purchasing this physical book you can also download the Kindle version **FREE** so you have it wherever you are. If you don't have a Kindle reader most smartphones have a Kindle app that you can download. Please see your Amazon account for details.

50 Wonderful attractions, including opening times, ticket prices, nearest car park or how to get there via public transport. Restaurants nearby, roughly how long you'll want there and what to expect (including details many other guides leave out). We even let you know if you can **save money by booking tickets in advance** (worth the price of this book alone)

Plus 10 of the **best activities** you can do in Seattle from Segways to biking and more.

The best shops and markets that you don't want to miss – Shopping in Pargue is fun and we've included some often missed places.

10 **Spectacular view points** – If you want to see incredible views of Seattle and take breath taking photos these are places you'll want to visit…..

Amazing **day trips outside Seattle** – Fancy exploring the wider area? We'll let you know the 'must see' destinations

This Seattle travel guide book will not guide you on hotel choices. I'm guessing you'll have the pre-booked that and use the online review sites to make your decision.

We wanted to give the maximum information we could on making your trip the most enjoyable by providing you with all the best attraction details and including information most other travel guide books leave out.

Enjoy your time in Seattle. Each attraction is listed by its popularity and rating on TripAdvisor.com (as of December 14) Although rankings change over time it's a great indication as to what a lot of people enjoy in Seattle.

That way if you only have a short time and you want to see the 'must see' destinations you probably want to visit the first few on the list. But if you are staying longer or want great attractions that many visitors miss look towards the end.

Attractions

Best View Points in Seattle

Activities in and around Seattle

Seattle's Best Restaurants

Top-Attractions

Space Needle

CC Image courtesy of Seattle Municipal Archives on Flickr

Opening / Closing Times
Monday – Thursday   10:00am – 11:00pm
Friday – Saturday   9:30am – 11:30pm
Sunday   9:30am – 11:00pm

Address / Contact Number –400 Broad St. Seattle,
WA 98109 / +1 206-905-2100
Website –http://www.spaceneedle.com

Ticket Price – Can you buy in advance? **–** Yes – tickets
priced at $12, $19 and $16 for general admission, space
needle and gardens, day and night admissions and a
flexi pass.
Average Visit Length? –Anywhere between half a day
to a whole day depending on which package is
purchased – average length 2-4 hours

Nearest car park –valet parking option at base of needle.
Nearest public transport stop – 167 towards Mercer St/Seattle Center

Attraction Summary – As the symbol of Seattle, the Space Needle boasts the best views of this striking American city. New York might be known as the city that never sleeps but Seattle is a hot contender with options to take in the beautifully breathtaking sights both day and night.

Open 365 days a year, the structure is one of the most easily recognized in the world. Erected in 1959, the observation deck stands at 605 feet and also contains a rotating restaurant. Built to withstand Seattle's changeable weather and able to combat winds and storms, the Space Needle is the must-see way to take in Seattle's gorgeous views.

As a landmark of the Specific Northwest, many recognize the Space Needle from the world of TV and film. Frasier is perhaps one of the most world-renowned shows to make use of the stunning sky tower.

Built in 1962 for the Seattle World Fair, over 2.3 million first came to see it, averaging at 20,000 people a day. It was once the tallest structure west of the Mississippi River and although it no longer remains so today, it still promises stellar views of Seattle's landscape and notable points of interest. Whether you spend an hour or an entire day and night taking in the sights and sounds of the city, the Space Needle is an essential stop.

Visitor Tips: It's worth scheduling in a trip at dusk to see the sun setting over the city.

Woodland Park Zoo

CC Image courtesy of Shannon Kringen on Flickr

Opening / Closing Times – Open daily between 9.30-5pm. Indoor exhibits close at 4pm. No entry after 4pm. Open daily except Christmas. May 1 to September 30 open until 7pm

Address / Contact Number –5500 Phinney Ave N, Seattle, WA 98103, United States/+1 206-548-2500

Website –www.zoo.org

Ticket Price – Can you buy in advance? Yes. Adult: $12.75 / Chilld $8.75 / Senior and disabled discount: $10.75 / Toddlers – free

Average Visit Length? – 5 hours

Nearest car park –5 zoo lots; Hippo, Flamingo, Penguin, Otter, Bear

Nearest public transport stop: Phinney Ave. N and N. 55th St.

Attraction Summary – Seattle's Woodland Park Zoo houses an array of exciting exhibits including Jaguar Cove, the Australasia Zone, the Temperate Forest and the African Savannah Exhibit, animal lovers can enjoy the sights and sounds of mammals, reptiles and amphibians, birds, invertebrates and plants. Representing 300 global species and housing more than 1,000 animals, visitors can see elephants, emus, Komodo dragons and cheetahs up close and personal whilst contributing to their conservation in the wild world beyond the zoo walls. A portion of every dollar spent goes towards saving animals in the natural world. The award winning zoo is comprised of 92 acres and will take a fair bit of exploring to see all the sights!

The zoo also consists of 35 endangered animal species and 5 threatened animal species, contains, 7,000 trees, 50,000 shrubs and herbs and 1,000 plant species lending it a variety that truly captivates the senses. Visitors can explore the animals of Africa one moment and delve into the mysteries of far-flung Asia the next making this the ideal stop for families and explorers alike. The Zoo's efforts with global conservation projects mark them out as hugely humanitarian with a respect and appreciation for the animals they house.

Visitor Tips: If you take the bus to the zoo and show your ticket at the booth, you'll get $2 off the regular admission price.

If you're visiting during the holidays, the zoo is open till 8.30pm for its annual winter holiday lights festival from November through January.

Museum of Flight

CC Image courtesy of Daniel Morrison on Flickr

Opening / Closing Times – 10am – 5pm, 7 days a week

Address / Contact Number –9404 East Marginal Way S, Seattle, WA 98108, United States/+1 206-764-5720

Website –http://www.museumofflight.org

Ticket Price – Can you buy in advance? Yes. Adults $19 – youths $11
Average Visit Length? – 4 hours
Nearest car park – free parking adjacent to museum
Nearest public transport stop –The bus stop is directly in front of the museum.

Attraction Summary – Seattle's Museum of Flight

embraces all things airborne and is designed to educate visitors about air and space. Exhibiting significant space and flight artefacts, scholars utilize the museum for research and visitors can peruse a glorious range of aircraft collections to take them back through time.

There's always something new on with an assortment of permanent exhibits including the striking 737 Airliner Theatre, Apollo 17 Mission Models, Cockpit experiences and decommissioned concords. Talk a walk down memory lane with stunning American and international flying machines.

There are also more unusual exhibits to explore including the ever-colourful Montgolfier Brother's Balloon, World War 1 Fighters and information detailing the inception of aviation.

As a private, non-profit museum, the museum of flight has been completely accredited by the American Alliance of Museums and remains the world's largest private museum dedicated to air and space.

400,000 visitors flock to the flight museum every year and it remains a captivating destination for those looking to explore America's historical involvement in space and up in the air. It's also an ideal destination for families looking for fun as well as space and aviation buffs owing to the educational and welcoming expanse of the museum making it well worth a day trip.

Visitor Tips: If you fancy arriving in style, the Museum has five spaces available for planes. That's right – you can literally fly in and park.

Seattle Symphony Orchestra

CC Image courtesy of D Coetzee on Flickr

Opening / Closing Times – Ticket office hours:
Monday–Friday: 10am–6pm
Saturday: 1pm–6pm

Address / Contact Number –200 University Street,
Seattle, WA (Downtown)/ 206-215-4747

Website –http://www.seattlesymphony.org/symphony/

Ticket Price – Can you buy in advance? Depends on
show – no specific price
Average Visit Length? – 2 hours
Nearest car park – Benaroya Hall, 200 University
Street, Seattle, WA 9810
Nearest public transport stop – University Street
Station

Attraction Summary – The Seattle Symphony is one of the city's most esteemed cultural jewels having delighted revelers with a taste for the finer things in life for years. Reaching over 315,000 music fans each and every year, the history of the Seattle Symphony has rendered it one of the most highly acclaimed performances in the world.

Lead by Music Director Ludovic Morlot, who retains his spot as one of his generations leading artists, the symphony has yielded 25,000 dedicated patrons, and presents 200 versatile performances to over 315,000 attendees. The Seattle Symphony has released over 140 recordings and achieved 12 Grammy nominations and 2 Emmy Awards making it a widely reputed hot house of class, talent and ultra-modern refinement.

With a spate of sensational new offerings for December, guests can enjoy a range of feasts for the ears in the modern architectural marvel that is the gloriously decadent Benaroya Hall. The esteemed Seattle Symphony brings the sights and sounds of splendid classical music to almost 50,000 people of all ages, helping classical music make a huge transformation in the lives of younger generations who may not yet have been acquainted with it and the older generations who have been raised on classical tunes. Breaching age gaps, the Seattle Symphony enables people of all tastes, ages and lifestyles to enjoy a flavor of classical music.

Visitor Tips: The Symphony holds special events through the year including holiday celebrations with pop up shops and special performances. Check the website when planning your trip.

Puzzle Break

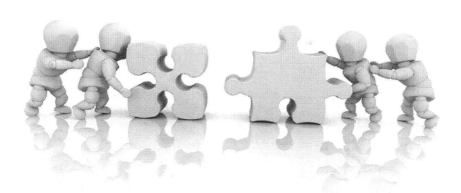

CC Image courtesy of Yoel Ben-Avraham on Flickr

Opening / Closing Times – Ticket office hours: Friday 7pm. Sat and Sunday 3pm – 7pm

Address / Contact Number –1423 10th Ave, Studio D, Seattle, WA 98122 /info@puzzlebreak.us

Website –http://www.puzzlebreak.us

Ticket Price – Can you buy in advance? –Yes varies, approx. $30
Average Visit Length? – 2 hours
Nearest car park –1420 10TH AV, SEATTLE, WA 98122
Nearest public transport stop –E Jefferson St and Broadway

Attraction Summary – For those that like a little adventure, Puzzle Break offers plenty of family fun. As a live action game, attendees have to escape a puzzle room with 11 others. Players have to locate the clues and hints of the room to solve a variety of puzzles and escape within the hour.

This attraction is both a staple for Seattle and a popular tourist attraction in San Francisco too, that encourages visitors to test their cunning and mental mobility with their families, friends, partners – in fact, just about anyone.

The world famous escapade offers players the opportunity to escape from a range of rooms including The Grimm Escape which really racks the brain up a notch. The key to success is communication with all gamers advised to keep in close contact and share their thoughts as they explore and solve puzzles.

Staff drop helpful hints too to keep the game ticking along and revelers are free to jump between games to gain a little inspiration. Utterly unique, communal and inspired, Puzzle Break reinforces friendships and helps secure new ones in a truly captivating way.

Take your kids, your wife, your date or your co-workers for a shared experience that you'll be talking about for years to come.

Visitor Tips: This is not an experience for the claustrophobic. Games are only available Friday – Sunday and they do sell out so book to avoid disappointment especially if you plan on visiting with a group.

Chihuly Garden and Glass

CC Image courtesy of Scott Costello on Flickr

Opening / Closing Times – 11am-7pm

Address / Contact Number –305 Harrison Street, Seattle, WA 98109 /+1 206-753-4940

Website –http://www.chihulygardenandglass.com

Ticket Price – Can you buy in advance? Yes. $12, $16 or $22

Average Visit Length? – 4 hours

Nearest car park – 401 5TH AV N, SEATTLE, WA 98109

Nearest public transport stop – 5th Ave N & Broad St

Attraction Summary – The brain child of Dale Chihuly, his stunningly contemporary glass works adorn the Seattle centre and have been enchanting guests since 1962, when the World's Fair completely remodeled the area and transformed it into a location of high acclaim. Designed to inspire and enthuse local and international visitors, the glass structures of Chihuly reflect the area's vibrant cultural community.

Situated side by side the Space Needle, visitors can easily kill two birds with one stone, taking in his inspirations and endless influences that have shone through in his striking works.

With eight galleries to choose between, the stunning piece de resistance that is the Glasshouse also offers verdant gardens to explore; there is no limit to how long you can spend perusing this magical expanse.

Chihuly is known for having pushed the boundaries of glass to create gorgeous crystalline structures and the Glasshouse showcases his work at its best. The 40 ft steel structure reflects the artists' love of conservatories making use of light and glass to create a beautiful suspended sculpture enthused with joyous oranges, yellows and reds.

A must see as the artwork changes with the light, meaning you will never see the same art twice! To get to grips with Chihuly's process, his theatre explains just how he set about his generous glass project.

Visitor Tips: The exhibit occasionally closes early for special events so check the website before travelling if you're hoping to visit in the late afternoon.

Safeco Field

CC Image courtesy of Amy Meredith on Flickr

Opening / Closing Times – 8.30-5.30

Address / Contact Number –1250 1st Ave S, Seattle, WA 98134, United States/206 346 4000

Website –http://seattle.mariners.mlb.com

Ticket Price – Can you buy in advance? Yes. Between $300 and $3,800 depending on seat.
Average Visit Length? – 4 hours
Nearest car park – 1520 OCCIDENTAL AV S, SEATTLE, WA 98134
Nearest public transport stop –King Street Station

Attraction Summary – Sports fans can't help but head

to Safeco Field, the baseball field with a retractable roof and home to Seattle's most popular team, the Seattle Mariners. Fans can catch any upcoming games and enjoy all of the hullaballoo and excitement that enthuses the air on game day.

With a range of delicious snacks and thirst quenching drinks available, the field is the ideal place for all game lovers to indulge in a truly memorable and remarkable sporting occasion at one of the world's most innovative arenas.

With a range of seating and ticket options available, baseball fans can opt for full season tickets or a versatile range of 20 game plans. Located in the SoDo district, Safeco Fields hones many of the features synonymous with 1990's builds including a retro-modern appeal that makes it an absolute must see.

The asymmetrical field design and brash brick exterior offset the lush natural grass field. With railroads, city streets and buildings all around, this baseball park also has an utterly urban touch that adds an intriguing mix to all games. You'll really feel like you're bang smack in the middle of the city, even whilst you watch the game. With a seating capacity of 47,476 individuals, you can bring as many buddies as you want and sit down to enjoy the all-American game.

Visitor Tips: It's much less hassle – and much quicker – to take public transport than to try and park on game days.

Kerry Park

CC Image courtesy of Tiffany Von Arnim on Flickr

Opening / Closing Times – Always open

Address / Contact Number –211 W Highland Dr, 98119/(206) 684-4075

Website –
http://www.seattle.gov/parks/park_detail.asp?ID=342

Ticket Price – Free

Average Visit Length? – 1 hour

Nearest car park – Street parking is available on W Highland Drive. Or Mercer Street Parking at 100 W MERCER ST, SEATTLE, WA 98119

Nearest public transport stop –Queen Ann Ave

Attraction Summary – Sometimes cities throw up freebies and when they do, it's hard to say no. It can be easy when you're in the middle of an urban jungle to forget about the natural world beyond but Kerry Park enables you to get back to basics offering irresistible views of both Elliott Bay and the Central City and also a tantalizing backdrop of Mount Rainier.

If you're handy with a camera or simply enjoy a leisurely stroll, there are plenty of vantage points to keep your camera occupied and endless opportunities to people watch and spy on the city. A gorgeous view to keep your camera ready for is sunset when hoards of photographs gather to catch the city in its most flattering light.

Night time is a great time to watch the park veiled with a magical light, spying the picturesque ferries lit up like lanterns and gliding across the dark waters. It's also the perfect place to see the Space Needle from afar jutting out and piercing the sky.

The park was given to the cities citizens by Mr and Mrs Kerry enabling all who visit the city to enjoy its striking appeal. As popular with locals as it is with tourists, Kerry Park is the perfect place to go to get back to basics.

Visitor Tips: If you plan to take a snapshot at sunset, arrive early as photographers line the walls as the sun goes down to capture Elliot Bay and Central City bathed in the last of the day's rays.

Pike Place Market

CC Image courtesy of Andrew E. Larsen on Flickr

Opening / Closing Times – Farmers: 9 am – 4 pm
Crafts Market: 10 am – 4 pm
Seafood: 7 am – 6 pm
Market Shops: 10 am – 6 pm
Restaurants: 6 am-1:30 am; hours vary by restaurant.

Address / Contact Number –85 Pike St, Seattle, WA
98101, United States/+1 206-682-7453

Website – http://www.pikeplacemarket.org/

Ticket Price – Free
Average Visit Length? – 1-2 hours
Nearest car park – 1615 WESTERN AV, SEATTLE, WA
98101
Nearest public transport stop – Pine Street

Attraction Summary – Overlooking Seattle's Elliot Bay waterfront, this gorgeous public market was founded in 1907 and is one of the oldest American farmers markets in action.

Offering a variety of goods, patrons can treat themselves to a range specialty foods, wholesome produce, fresh fish, meat and dairy, and imported and artisan goods as well as a variety of craft goods. Drawing a huge crowd of farmers, merchants, crafters and of course buyers every year, the market is mixed with a lively infusion of locals and tourists.

With a variety of levels available, the market consists of an assortment of high end and normal restaurants, comic stores, collectable shops and antique dealers and also houses one of Seattle's oldest shops. Available all year round, the options change on a daily basis making this market an exhilarating and exciting experience for all attendees.

To see the real heart and soul of Seattle, the market is a great place to start. Immerse yourself into the very centre of Seattle life, rub shoulders with the lovely locals and snare yourself some dynamic new goods. Open daily and free to attend, the Pike Place market is a Seattle staple that isn't going out of fashion any time soon.

Visitor Tips: Snack as you go and bring a bag to gather picnic supplies. The market is busy early on so it's worth setting your alarm to grab the freshest produce.

Waterfront Market

CC Image courtesy of Gene Bisbee on Flickr

Opening / Closing Times – All day

Address / Contact Number –1301 Alaskan Way, Seattle, WA 98101, United States/+1 206-684-4075

Website – No official website
http://www.yelp.co.nz/biz/waterfront-park-seattle

Ticket Price – Free
Average Visit Length? – 1-2 hours
Nearest car park – 50 UNIVERSITY ST, SEATTLE, WA 98101
Nearest public transport stop – Pine Street

Attraction Summary – A fun free family attraction has to be waterfront park. Whether you grab a yummy meal from Pike Place market and need somewhere quiet to sit down and have a meal or whether you feel like people watching and taking in the sights, the Waterfront Park provides stunning views of Seattle city.

For gorgeous views of the nearby Ferris wheel and the ferries bobbing on the water, Waterfront Park cannot be beaten. There are plenty of nearby seafood restaurants to partake of and an endless array of quirky shops.

Just the right mixture of locals and tourists makes this an exciting stop. It's also a great starting point for a ferry trip to any of the neighboring islands or for those flocking further afield, to Canada! An ideal place to get close to the water even amidst the urban sprawl, this is the space for lovers who want to take in idyllic scenery, groups of friends who want to enjoy a beer by the waterfront or families who want to make precious memories.

It's also a great place to go to catch the sunrise or sunset as soon as you can with views of the city that immediately light up. Make sure you have your camera ready.

Visitor Tips: As with most markets it pays to arrive early so you have your pick of produce. It's worth stopping here first if you have a day of sightseeing planned and picking up snacks and picnic supplies before you set off.

The market is right next door to the great wheel so kill two birds with one stone and head their next.

Seattle Great Wheel

CC Image courtesy of T.Tseng on Flickr

Opening / Closing Times – 11am-10pm – mon-thurs. Friday 11am-12am. Sat 10 am-12am. Sun 10am-10pm

Address / Contact Number –1301 Alaskan Way, Seattle, WA 98101, United States/+1 206-623-8607

Website – http://www.seattlegreatwheel.com
Ticket Price – Can you buy in advance? No. $13 adult. $8.50 child.
Average Visit Length? – 1 hour
Nearest car park – 50 UNIVERSITY ST, SEATTLE, WA 98101
Nearest public transport stop – Pine Street

Attraction Summary – Seattle's great wheel is well

known as a treasured spot and is one of Seattle's most historic landscapes. Perfectly situated by the Waterfront Park, guests can tick off two stunningly essential visitors' spots and indulge their inner child with a high up view of the city of Seattle.

The idea way to take in Seattle's superb sights, the Seattle great wheel took less than a year to build and was the brainchild of American businessman Hal Griffith. He had dreamed of building a Ferris wheel in the city for over 30 years and decided to build one on his very own pier.

The wheel has only been open to the public since 2012 but remains an endearingly popular tourist destination for loyal locals and tourists in town. It's the very largest observation wheel located on the west coast, and contains 42 fully-enclosed gondolas including VIP gondolas for those willing to pay a little extra. VIP gondolas include a glass bottom view for true panoramic views, leather seats, and a stereo system.

The wheel can house up to 300 passengers and is open all year round, making it the perfect way to see the city in style. Make sure you bring your camera because these views are a once in a lifetime experience.

Visitor Tips: The wheel is next to the Waterfront Market so head their first and then go to the wheel.

Winter hours operate from Sept – June. If you wrap up warm, it's worth visiting late on (operation stops at 10pm to see the city lit up).

Seattle Aquarium

CC Image courtesy of David Davies on Flickr

Opening / Closing Times – 9.30am-5.00pm

Address / Contact Number –1483 Alaskan Way, Seattle, WA 98101, United States/+1 206-386-4300

Website – http://www.seattleaquarium.org

Ticket Price – Can you buy in advance? Yes. Adults $21.95, Youth (4 – 12) $14.95
Average Visit Length? – 3 hours
Nearest car park – 1422 ALASKAN WY, SEATTLE, WA

98101

Nearest public transport stop —Waterfront, Alaskan Way, in front of the Aquarium

Attraction Summary — Immerse yourself in perfect family fun by exploring Seattle's inspirational aquarium. Located on Pier 59 on the waterfront, you and your family can explore an endless array of exhibits designed to flaunt as well as educate onlookers about the wondrous underwater world. With a range of ocean oddities to explore, visitors can also sneak a look at Washington's waters. Housing underwater critters from all over the world, visitors can see an assortment of corals, cowfish, seahorses and harlequin shrimp up close and personal.

Their beautiful open air exhibit introduces visitors to a wide range of native and not so native birds whilst kids and adults alike can explore tide pools and find out more about local fish species. With an array of fabulously exotic creatures on display, it's possible to witness the daily octopus feeding which is not to be missed if you're a fan of such beautifully bizarre life forms. For a fully immersive experience, guests can surround themselves by the sea in the underwater dome for an unmissable up-close view, look for sharks and orcas and check out a range of marine mammals including seals.

Visitor Tips: If you're visiting with kids, don't miss Sea Strolling which takes place before the aquarium officially opens to the public. Begins 9am on Sundays. If you're visiting on a Sunday, there is free metered street parking.

Seattle Children's Museum

CC Image courtesy of William Prost on Flickr

Opening / Closing Times – 10am – 5pm

Address / Contact Number –305 Harrison Street
Seattle, WA 98109/ Box office: 206-441-1768 option 3

Website – http://thechildrensmuseum.org

Ticket Price – Can you buy in advance? Yes. $8.25
Average Visit Length? –
Nearest car park – 401 5TH AV N, SEATTLE, WA 98109
Nearest public transport stop –Mercer St

Attraction Summary – If you're in town visiting the
Space Needle, Seattle's Children's Museum is a mere
150 steps away and well worth stopping in for. Designed
with kids in mind, adults and big kids alike can also find
a lot of fun here, although children and parents are most

definitely the intended audience! With a range of exciting exhibits stretching over 22,000 square feet, a world of imagination and adventure lies around every corner.

There's a variety of options to explore including cog city, discovery bay, fort adventure and global village. Children can let their creative juices flow in the imagination studio and find out more about essential occupations in the neighborhood.

The sound transit station and storytelling circle captivate children's senses and the festival of light and program centre has plenty to keep kids occupied. This is a one stop shop for all things childhood and ranks as one of kid's favorite things to do in the city of Seattle. Explosions of color, light, sound and sights help children's imaginations run wild and yours might run a little rampant too.

Encapsulating the best of childhood, this family friendly space offers every exciting activity known to man in one child friendly environment to help your child learn, play and make friends.

Visitor's Tips: The Children's Museum is only a few steps away from the Space Needle.

Kids young and old are likely to get carried away here so allow plenty of time for your visit.

Asian Art Museum

CC Image courtesy of Kent Wang on Flickr

Opening / Closing Times – WEDNESDAY:10AM-5PM
THURSDAY:10AM-9PM
FRIDAY-SUNDAY:10AM-5PM

Address / Contact Number –Volunteer Park, 1400
East Prospect Street Seattle, WA 98112 / Tel:
206.654.3100 & 206.344.5267

Website –
http://www.seattleartmuseum.org/visit/asian-art-
museum

Ticket Price -varies for exhibit
Average Visit Length? – 3hr
Nearest car park –Street parking is unrestricted
between 14th Ave E and 15th S Ave E S Side
Nearest public transport stop –Broad St

Attraction Summary – Seattle has a large Asian
population and now visitors can explore a stunning array

of gorgeous pieces procured from the Asian world and inspired by Asian artists. Set in the verdant Volunteer Park, this picturesque museum houses a striking assortment of prestigious pieces to capture the colors and vibe of Asia.

The museums entrance is decorated with lush greenery and the inside fuses classic and modern works for a true walkthrough of Asian history and culture. As a relatively small museum, it's perfect for those trying to pack a lot into a day or who want something to do before they head home.

Designed in an art deco style, a variety of permanent and temporary exhibits are on display and on Thursdays, the museum is free for all making it perfect for those who don't want to break the bank. With free parking and a plethora of art from Japan, Korea, China and India, outside offers unbeatable views also, with the Space Needle firmly in view.

With an idyllic location, guests can easily amble around the Asian Art music at a leisurely place taking in the sight in their own time. Whether you go alone or bring a crowd, there's more than enough to help you whittle away a day.

Visitor Tips: The museum is closed Mondays. Open late night till 9pm. The first Thursday of each month is free to all. The first Saturday of each month is free for families.

Experience Music Project Museum

CC Image courtesy of Razvan Orendovici on Flickr

Opening / Closing Times – 10am-5pm

Address / Contact Number –325 5th Ave N, Seattle, WA 98109, United States/+1 206-770-2700

Website – http://www.empmuseum.org

Ticket Price – Can you buy in advance? Yes, $18
Average Visit Length? –3hr
Nearest car park – Street parking is available at the museum. A parking lot is located by the building, at 5th Avenue N and Harrison Street
Nearest public transport stop – 5th ave

Attraction Summary – Seattle's EMP museum remains one of the world's most innovative, non-profit museums dedicated to contemporary culture. Celebrating risk, fresh ideas and ultra-modern inspiration, this is a museum with its finger on the pulse that will certainly leave you feeling invigorated and enlivened. This museum will certainly get you thinking offering endless educational experiences, interactive installations and captivating histories.

There are a variety of exhibitions to choose from including the Indie Game revolution, Game of Thrones ascend the wall, We are 12, Spectacle the Music Video, Fantasy: Worlds of Myth and Magic, the hits of Jimmy Hendrix, science fiction icons and Nirvana: Taking Punk to the Masses.

All the best of popular culture is showcased here for all to see. For some it will be a walk down memory lane and for others a visceral explosion of life and color.

Turning museums on their head, this experience is a must for fans and popular culture devotees who get to see their most treasured idols celebrated in a hugely iconic way.

Ideal for those who avoid conventional museums like the plague or simply want to dabble in something fresh and funky, the Experience Music Project museum is one you won't want to forget in a hurry.

Visitor Tips: The museum holds a variety of events through the year so check the events calendar on the site before you book tickets.

Sky City at the Space Needle

CC Image courtesy of Dan Ox on Flickr

Opening / Closing Times – 11am-2.45pm /5-9.45pm

Address / Contact Number –400 Broad St, Seattle, WA 98109, United States / +1 206-905-2100

Website – http://www.spaceneedle.com/information/

Average Visit Length? **–**2hr
Nearest car park –parking available at the needle
Nearest public transport stop – Broad street

Attraction Summary – Originally referred to as the 'eye of the needle' Sky City is a decadent rotating restaurant situated on the top tier of the Seattle Space Needle.

The 14 foot deep carousel contains the lucky diners who get to enjoy first class food whilst taking in the devastatingly jaw-dropping panoramic views of the city. Seated up in the sky, diners can enjoy first rate views of the sea and all of Seattle's splendors whilst savoring mouth-watering cuisine.

Expect to dine for brunch, lunch and dinner. Dress code has to be family friendly but otherwise glamorous, professional and ultra casual attire are all welcomed.

Eaters can sample grilled gulf prawns, hazelnut crusted French toast, mountain huckleberry pancakes, and finish with deliriously delicious seasonal cobbler and chocolate cheesecake parfait.

Lunching diners can enjoy a plethora of prestigiously prepared eats including wild salmon fritters, American burgers and chop chop salad.

Finally those looking to dine during the evening or to celebrate a special event can tuck into platefuls of burrata and bresola, ahi tuna, jidori chicken and enhancements such as duck fat frites and young Portobello mushrooms.

There's a kid's menu available too so all of the family can eat in an elitist way – perfect for a once in a lifetime trip to Seattle or to commemorate a special occasion.

Visitor Tips: Reservations are required and the restaurant is often fully booked so call early to be assured of a table. Open for brunch and lunch, Sky City comes into its own at dinner when the twinkling lights of Seattle are laid out beneath you.

Botanical Gardens

CC Image courtesy of jc.winkler on Flickr

Opening / Closing Times – 7am - 9pm

Address / Contact Number – **3015 54th St NW Seattle, WA 98107 / 206-783-7059**

Website –
http://www.gardenvisit.com/garden/carl_s_english_jr_b otanical_garden

Ticket Price –Free
Average Visit Length? –2hr
Nearest car park –Pike Place
Nearest public transport stop –NE 55

Attraction Summary – The Carl S. English Jr. Botanical Gardens is a garden fashioned between the locks connecting Puget Sound to Lakes Union and Washington, cultivated by the man himself. As a revered botanist and horticulturist, English was able to expertly craft beauteous gardens in the style of an English estate garden. Having discovered three rare plants, including the fameflower, bitter root and spring beauty before his retirement, the garden is a verdant, flourishing expanse of beauty and magic ideal for all.

If you're looking to escape the urban sprawl that is the city, taking a stroll through the botanical gardens is the ideal place to relax in complete tranquility. The garden consists of over 500 species and 1,500 varieties of plants from all around the world to encapsulate the most stunning offerings available. Plant lovers, nature enthusiasts and those looking to escape will enjoy the splendor and beauty of one of Seattle's most beauteous and highly treasured locations. Often housing weddings and other celebrations, you'll soon see why with views to die for and stunning flower formations that reflect a true English garden – there's even a gorgeous assembly of roses amidst all of the wild fauna to give your nose a treat. That's one thing about the botanical gardens – they smell absolutely amazing!

Visitor Tips: Lunch time is a great time to visit – especially if you've been running around exploring the city. Set aside 30 mins in the early afternoon to relax and unwind.

The gardens are located by the Hiram M. Chittenden Locks so you can kill two birds with one stone and tick both attractions off your to do list.

Ye Olde Curiosity Shop

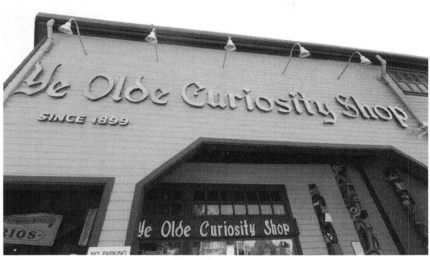

CC Image courtesy of Jason Baker on Flickr

Opening / Closing Times – 10-6pm

Address / Contact Number –

1001 Alaskan Way, Seattle, WA 98104, United States /+1 206-682-5844

Website –http://yeoldecuriosityshop.com/

Ticket Price –na
Average Visit Length? –30m
Nearest car park –**1101 WESTERN AV, SEATTLE, WA 98101**
Nearest public transport stop –Alaskan Way

Attraction Summary – Tucked away on Alaskan Way is Seattle's intriguing 'Ye Olde Curiosity Shop'.

Combining an eccentric store and a marvelous museum, the shop was first utilized as a trading post back during the era of the gold rush. The shop has then gone on to procure a vast array of oddities such as shrunken heads, two headed goats, mummies, paintings drawn on pinheads and the Lord's Prayer entirely reconstructed on a single grain of rice. The family oriented endeavor is into its 5th generation and in that time has assembled endless curiosities from all over the globe.

Selling a range of novelty gifts, it's the ideal place to pick up an utterly one of a kind present as well as homemade fudge and authentic Native American artwork. For those who like eccentricities and oddities, the Curiosity Shop is a truly captivating find where you can lose hours of time exploring all of the wonders on offer.

A true place of fantasy, mystery, intrigue and freakishness, you can also see the jewelery of a real circus giant and the cutlery of cannibals and a plethora of further peculiarities. You won't believe what you'll see, so we'll keep a few things secret for you!

Visitor Tips: Save a few of your souvenir shopping requirements for a trip here and pick up something a little different for friends back home.

5th Avenue Theatre

CC Image courtesy of Blake Handley on Flickr
Opening / Closing Times – 10-6pm

Address / Contact Number –1308 5th Ave, Seattle, WA 98101, United States
+1 206-625-1900
Website –https://www.5thavenue.org/

Ticket Price – Can you buy in advance? Yes, prices vary
Average Visit Length? –2-3hr

Nearest car park –Pike Place
Nearest public transport stop –5th ave

Attraction Summary – Theatre lovers flock to the 5th Avenue Theatre to see all of their favourite shows. New York's Broadway and London's West End are typically thought of as the perfect theatre haunts but 5th avenue has a little special spark that makes it a much loved Seattle staple. Whether you're looking for a sporting event, a travelling Broadway show fresh out of the Big Apple, comedy shows, games and national tours, you'll find all of that and more behind these hallowed doors.

With performances from some of the world's most acclaimed bands, pop stars and musicians; you can catch a range of spellbinding shows that will make your trip to Seattle unforgettable. There's always something new on to suit all the family.

It's a chance to sit down and be entertained by some true up and coming stars and a few that have already cemented themselves on the Hollywood walk of fame. From the NFL to Taylor Swift, NBA to the NHL and The Book of Mormon to Disney on Ice, you can catch it all for an outing with friends, family, lovers and loved ones. Celebrate in style or see what's going on this season at Seattle's famous 5th avenue theatre.

Visitor Tips: Shows change regularly. There are lots of festive performances around the holidays so check the website before travelling to find best available seats.

The Kubota Garden

CC Image courtesy of Jake Jacobson on Flickr

Opening / Closing Times – 6am-10pm

Address / Contact Number –*9817 55th Ave S, 98118 / (206) 684-4075*

Website – http://www.kubotagarden.org

Ticket Price –Can you buy in advance? Free entry

Average Visit Length? –1hr

Nearest car park –Street parking is unrestricted on 55th Ave S Between Renton Ave S And S Ryan St W Side

Nearest public transport stop –Pike Place

Attraction Summary – The Kubota Garden consists of over 20 magical acres that immerse wanderers in the totality of nature. Free and utterly expansive, there is so much to see that you could get lost for days traversing the gardens. Whether you're visiting in winter or summer, the gardens still look beautiful and wonderfully atmospheric.

You'd be advised to bring your camera because there are some stunning sights to capture. Having been around for over 90 years, the gardens remain well-maintained and offer a great retreat from the hustle and bustle of the city. Whether you fancy a wander, a romantic stroll, a place to meditate serenely or the ideal spot to practice a morning yoga session, these gardens have it all.

Occupied by a range of colorful local characters and exploring tourists, the atmosphere of the gardens is always electric with plenty of places to retreat for a little peace and quiet. There's an endless array of trees, plants and shrubbery and gorgeous water structures teaming with koi.

With an array of walking trails available, you can explore for hours and completely lose track of time. Whether you've been to Japan 100 times or never, escape into far flung Asia in these gorgeously mercurial gardens.

Visitor Tips: Although entrance to the gardens is free of charge, donations are encouraged. This goes towards park maintenance and special exhibits such as the ishigaki, which is part of new terrace works.

Seattle Theatre

CC Image courtesy of Blake Handley on Flickr

Opening / Closing Times – 9-5pm

Address / Contact Number *–911 Pine St, Seattle, WA 98101, United States*

Website –http://www.stgpresents.org/paramount

Ticket Price – Can you buy in advance? Yes, ticket price varies
Average Visit Length? –3hr
Nearest car park –Pine Market Parking

Nearest public transport stop –Pine Street

Attraction Summary – With a choice of three, Seattle's Paramount, Moore and Neptune theatres is a series of non-profits art organizations. They aim to help performance and arts related education enriching whilst ensuring that Seattle's history is preserved for all visitors and locals alike to experience. They believe that the world can be inspired, expanded and challenged through various arts. With 500 events presented annually, theatre goers have a well-rounded range to choose between. There's a plethora of lectures, theatre productions, concerts, film and community and education programs as well as a variety of further enrichment programs.

The theatre's success is the result of a hugely expansive collaborative effort between patrons, volunteers, foundations, donors, partner organizations and of course, the variety of artists and performers on show. The three theatres are notorious pillars of Seattle society with the Paramount theatre touted as 'Seattle's most opulent movie palace.' The stunningly grand decadence of the theatres makes it enough of a show all by itself. Fans can catch a variety of promising, highly entertaining performances including Gaelic Storm, John Oliver, Cold Specks and Smallpools & Magic Man and with the option for premium seating, you can enjoy all the views and performers in style up close.

Visitor Tips: Splurge on premier seating for a truly VIP experience

Saint James Cathedral

CC Image courtesy of Wonderlane on Flickr

Opening / Closing Times – 7.30-6pm

Address / Contact Number –*804 9th Ave, Seattle, WA 98104, United States+1 206-622-3559*

Website –<u>http://www.stjames-cathedral.org/</u>

Ticket Price – Can you buy in advance? Free entry

Average Visit Length? –1-2hr

Nearest car park –910 8TH AV, SEATTLE, WA 98104

Nearest public transport stop –1st Avenue

Attraction Summary – To truly take in the culture and sweeping history of Seattle, a visit to Saint James Cathedral is an absolute must. The Cathedral has a vast history spanning 100 years. Initiated in 1850, the cathedral showcases an exciting smattering of events including the Children's Faith Formation, A Christmas Carol reading and a variety of mass and penance services.

The striking cathedral is a true Seattle landmark and is the mother church of the Archdiocese of Seattle. The Cathedral also houses some riveting art and music with an extensive stained glass collection from Charles Connick and a Madonna and Child flanked by six saints constructed by Florentine artist Neri di Bicci.

Containing a candlelit shrine to the Blessed Virgin Mary, the interior is spacious and immaculately cared for and harks back to stunning European churches of old. Music and prayer sessions reverberate throughout the room creating a truly poignant atmosphere. For an absolutely spiritual experience, this is the ideal place to venture either alone or with friends and family. The grounds surrounding the cathedral are lush and ideal for a little respite from the non-stop modern world. A place of peace, calm and serenity, make this a stop on your itinerary.

Visitor Tips: Mass is held on Saturdays at 8:15 am with "Vigil" 5:30 pm., On Sundays at 8, 10, 12, & 5:30 pm and Weekdays at   8:15 am & 5:30 pm and on

Pioneer Square

CC Image courtesy of Ming-yen Hsu on Flickr

Opening / Closing Times – 24-7

Address / Contact Number –310 1st Ave S, Seattle, WA 98104, United States

Phone:+1 206-667-0687

Website –http://www.pioneersquare.org/

Ticket Price – Can you buy in advance? Free entry
Average Visit Length? – 2hr
Nearest car park –305 1ST AV S, SEATTLE, WA 98104
Nearest public transport stop –4th ave

Attraction Summary – Pioneer Square is the ideal place to lose yourself in Seattle city. If you're a fan of people watching, leisurely strolls and exploring unusual finds, then Pioneer Square is the perfect place to do so. Located in the historical heart of Seattle, centuries of history will unravel around you as you pound the pavements of these story-telling streets. There's a huge range of things to do meaning that you can spend hours in a world of imagination.

There's a plethora of exciting eats to consume from all four corners of the globe, an usual array of intriguing shops and stores, perfect for grabbing yourself a souvenir and beautiful boutiques to whittle away a few hours browsing.

There's also a range of sporting events and exciting night life options, whether your preference is a heavy night on the tiles or a romantic meal for two.

Taking a wander through Pioneer Square is indisputably the best way to take in the sights and sounds of Seattle. Brush shoulders with the locals, having been around for over 100 years. You'll fall in love with Seattle in a whole new way so make sure you dedicate a huge chunk of time to exploring all that the city has to offer.

Visitor Tips: For a great atmosphere on game days, head to Pioneer Square. There are no less than 19 sports bars to sample.

Sky View Observatory

CC Image courtesy of Joe Wolf on Flickr

Opening / Closing Times –10am-8.30pm

Address / Contact Number **–**701 5th Ave, Seattle, WA 98104, United States / 1 206-386-5564

Website – http://www.skyviewobservatory.com

Ticket Price – Can you buy in advance? Yes, Adults $12.50. Children (6 – 12) $9
Average Visit Length? –2hr
Nearest car park –5th ave
Nearest public transport stop –4th ave

Attraction Summary – Standing at just under 1,000 feet, the Sky View observatory provides you with the tallest viewpoint west of the Mississippi. The all-encompassing 360 panoramic view packs in all of the best sights, including the Cascade Mountains, Elliot Bay, the Space Needle, Mt Rainier, Bellevue, Mt Baker, the Olympic Mountains and of course, the exquisite city itself. The 76 story building covers 1.5 million square feet and is attired in tempered smoked glass and Carnelian granite.

With other 8,800 windows, 2,100 heat pumps, 6 escalators and 48 elevators, it has taken over from the Space Needle as being the highest point of the city. Able to withstand Seattle's extremes of weather, the observatory remains one of the safest, secure buildings in the Pacific North west.

Make sure to catch the view around sunrise or sunset for a truly magical view of the city. Whatever the weather, rain or shine, the atmosphere at the top of the observatory is always liable to change meaning that no two days are the same.

This is an ideal trip for those brand new to the city who want to see everything on offer. It's also perfect to celebrate your last night in Seattle or for those who are only in time for a short while and want a bird's eye view of everything.

Visitor Tips: The highest Starbucks in the world can be found at the Sky View Observatory, in the Sky Lobby on the 40th floor. Now that's a brew with a view!

Washington State Ferries

CC Image courtesy of Hammerin Man on Flickr
Opening / Closing Times –

Address / Contact Number –

Website – http://www.wsdot.wa.gov/ferries/

Ticket Price – Can you buy in advance? Yes Fare
depends on terminal and destination
Average Visit Length? – NA
Nearest car park – NA
Nearest public transport stop – NA

Attraction Summary – No trip to Washington would
be complete without a short ferry trip. Synonymous with
Washington, many clamour at parks and beaches to
catch a glimpse of a floating ferry but why not ride on
one for real? Taking off from countless terminals, you

can look back on Seattle from the sea. Sunrise and sunset ferries really promote promising views and you could be in one of the many snaps taken from the shore by a hoard of photographers!

For picture postcard views, take to the sea and get to know Seattle by water. It's also possible to evade peak times and agonizingly long queues with a feature that promotes the best times to travel. You can opt to travel to the San Juan Islands, Port Townsend, Fauntleroy, Port Defiance and Southworth amongst a range of other options.

Taking to the water in a ferry not only promises great views but also a thoroughly unforgettable experience of Seattle the way it's meant to be seen. If you've tried the panoramic views offered by the Space Needle and the Sky View observatory, then why not see a side to Seattle often concealed by booking yourself a fun and fabulous ferry right from a whole new angle.

Alki Beach

CC Image courtesy of Chas Redmond Flickr

Opening / Closing Times – 4am-11.30pm

Address / Contact Number –*1702 Alki Ave SW, Seattle, WA 98116, United States+1 206-684-4075*

Website –
http://www.seattle.gov/parks/park_detail.asp?ID=445

Ticket Price – Can you buy in advance? Free entry

Average Visit Length? –4hr
Nearest car park –on street parking
Nearest public transport stop –West Seattle Bridge

Attraction Summary – If you fancy packing a beach into your trip of Seattle then Alki beach is the place to be. Located in West Seattle, you can enjoy the sights and sounds of Seattle from the shore. With sumptuous views of Elliot Bay, the Olympic mountains and the entirely of Seattle, this is one of the most picturesque spots to catch the sunrise.

There's a plethora of restaurants to hand if you fancy grabbing a quick snack before your beach stroll or venture into the lapping waves with fish and chip fare, and a range of local eateries. There's even a Starbucks and a Sally's if you fancy a perky pick me up coffee! Happy hour is the perfect time to dine if you fancy a discount.

The beach is full of wanderers, the occasional swimmer (although the water is chilly!), skateboarders, bikers and rollerbladers. Summer is the best time to visit as its the time when all beaches the world over come to life and Seattle is no different. At night time Seattle is all lit up and makes for a great sight, especially for that someone special. Make sure you take your camera because the views from here can be absolutely breathtaking.

Visitor Tips: Head to the beach as the sun goes down for happy hour cocktails and a beautiful sunset view

REI Climbing Pinnacle

CC Image courtesy of Keith Caswell on Flickr

Opening / Closing Times – Fridays: 1:30pm-6:30pm (Walk-ins only), Saturdays: 11am-7pm, Sundays: 11am-7pm or 11am-12:30pm

Address / Contact Number –222 Yale Ave N, Seattle, WA 98109, United States / 1 206-223-1944

Website – http://www.rei.com/stores/seattle/climb-class.html

Ticket Price – Can you buy in advance? Yes. $25- $30
Average Visit Length? – 1hr
Nearest car park –On site
Nearest public transport stop –Denny Way and Stewart Street

Attraction Summary – If you want to get your adrenaline pumping and explore Seattle's great outdoors then get yourself to the REI climbing pinnacle. Operated by the REI outdoor school, the pinnacle can be seen from blocks away just tempting you to give it a go.

Seattle is all about seeing the sights from up high and reaching the top is another great way to look back over the stylish city, this time with your blood pumping! All climbs include essential climbing garb and an outdoor school staff belayer. You can choose between a 15 and 30 minute slot but you can also opt for open climbs or climb classes as well as group and private climbs.

Standing at 65 ft tall, the pinnacle climb is an iconic feature of Seattle and has been ever since REI opened their flagship store in 1996. On clear days, the view stretches far and showcases Seattle's marvelous mountain rages but you can also catch gorgeous glimpses of the city that make it all worthwhile. Push yourself to the limit for a fun and fabulous day.

There's something very enjoyable about partaking in climbing the pinnacle! Go solo or drag your friends, family and co-workers with you; there's an option for all at the pinnacle.

Visitor Tips: The perfect Sunday morning activity, book an AM climb to blow the cobwebs away after a Saturday night in the City and then head to brunch downtown.

Gas Works Park

CC Image courtesy of Wildcat Dunny on Flickr

Opening / Closing Times – N/A

Address / Contact Number – *2101 N Northlake Way, 98103 / (206) 684-4075*
Website –
http://www.seattle.gov/parks/park_detail.asp?ID=293

Ticket Price – Can you buy in advance? Free entry
Average Visit Length? – 1 hour
Nearest car park – Available on site. 2101 N Northlake Way, 98103

Nearest public transport stop – Wallingford Ave N & N 35th St

Attraction Summary – An urban park with a difference, this is another great green space in the heart of the city. The major landmark and focal point of this city park is the very unusual – and very cool – industrial plant which has been repurposed as a children's play area. The play barn has been filled with brightly painted and decommissioned machinery

If you can drag yourself away from the rusty old iron works turned adventure playground, the aptly named Gas Works Parks is also home to a pretty lake and picnic area with benches and a grill. There's lots of space to explore and hiking and cycling trails, making it a pleasant interlude for all the family on warmer days.

The park is also a popular picture spot and offers panoramic views of the Seattle skyline. After clambering over the gas works and picnicking in the snack area, grab your camera and take a few snap shots to enjoy later.

You've never seen gnarly old industry so at one with nature which is why Gas Works park attracts such a variety of tourists and residents day after day.

There's ample parking available on site and good public transport links if you don't want to bring the car.

Visitor Tips: Locals flock to the large hill to fly kites – grab yourself a kite and give it a go or just watch the natives strut their stuff on weekends.

University of Washington

CC Image courtesy of Ming-yen Hsu on Flickr

Opening / Closing Times – 08.30 – 5.00

Address / Contact Number – *Visitor's Centre* 022 *Odegaard, Seattle, WA 98195-550* / 206-543-9198

Website – http://www.washington.edu/

Ticket Price – NA

Nearest car park – Garage at 15th Ave NE, NE 41st St

Nearest public transport stop –8th Avenue and Stewart Street

Attraction Summary – American universities house a certain nostalgia for many non-American citizens. Having grown up on TV shows that promote sweeping, vast school grounds that seem to go on forever, most people want to catch sight of an actual American university;

they seem to have become almost a little mythical! As one of the world's most prestigious universities, Washington has it's finger firmly on the pulse, launching young people into exciting futures, and dedicating time to research and scholarships.

Every year, 54,000 students step through the doors and you'll easily see why. The grounds are absolutely immaculate and look like something out of a fairy tale. Lined with cherry blossoms and verdant green grass, the architecture of the university sits snugly behind this green expanse. The views are truly breathtaking and not to be missed. Peruse the campus on foot to catch student life in action; kids hurrying to classes, revising out on the fields and hanging out with their friends.

A truly spellbinding experience both inside and out, the best views are in spring when the blossoms are in full bloom but the university remains impressive all year round and is a definite stop off spot for anyone in town. Make sure you add it to your to-do list.

Visitor Tips: Don't plan a visit without checking out the campus calendar first. If you can time your trip coincide your trip with a Husky game or arts event then it's advisable to do so. The University has a thriving arts project with thought provoking lectures. A trip on game days will give you firsthand experience of what American school life is really all about. Highly recommended!

Cinerama

CC Image courtesy of Andrew Hitchcock on Flickr

Opening / Closing Times – varies depending on movie times

Address / Contact Number –

2100 4th Ave, Seattle, WA 98121, United States
+1 206-448-6680

Website – http://www.cinerama.com

Ticket Price –Can you buy in advance? Yes, price varies
Average Visit Length? – 2-3 hr
Nearest car park – Warwick Hotel, 2020 4th Ave, Seattle, WA 98121
Nearest public transport stop – Westlake & Virginia Streetcar

Attraction Summary – It's been voted the world's best cinema so Cinerama is nothing to shake a stick at. For non-American's, a trip to an all-American cinema is an absolute must. Owned by Microsoft's co-founder Paul Allen, the cinema has recently reopened and had a few nips and tucks that have made it even greater.

Referred to as Seattle's most epic movie experience, movie goers can catch all the latest movie releases boosted with Dolby Atmos sound, laser projected seating, wonderfully comfortable seating, upgraded seating options and a plethora of local wines, beers and ciders and tasty eats and snacks to keep you full. The theatre itself is utterly eye catching and houses original costumes from a range of highly acclaimed movies including Star Wars, Blade Runner and the Batman movies. For any film fanatic, this cinema is an absolute must see at least once in your life and especially if you are only in Seattle for a short time.

Decadently delicious snacks include yummy chocolate popcorn, Theo chocolate candies, Full Tilt ice cream, pretzels and sausages to stop your stomach from rumbling during the show. Pull up a pew, grab a beer and some popcorn and relax in captivating surroundings. This is one of the best things to do in Seattle.

Seattle Pinball Museum

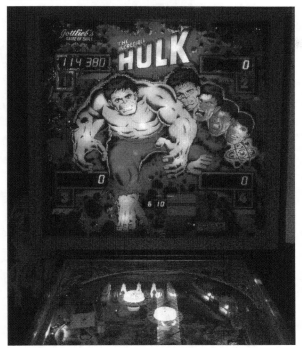

CC Image courtesy of J. Nathan Matias on Flickr

Opening / Closing Times Tuesday, Wednesday, Thursday: 2pm - 9pm Friday: 2pm - midnight Saturday: 11am - midnight Sunday: 11am - 9pm Monday: closed Closed Thanksgiving, Christmas and New Year's Day

Address / Contact Number –
508 Maynard Ave S, Seattle, WA 98104, United States / 1 206-623-0759

Website – http://pacificpinball.org/

Ticket Price – Can you buy in advance? Adults $15, under 16 $7.50
Average Visit Length? – 2-3 hours

Nearest car park – 5th Avenue N and Harrison Street
Nearest public transport stop – Westlake Center
Station: 5th Avenue and Pine Street

Attraction Summary – The Seattle Pinball Museum is a bit of an all-American institution and an absolute must see. Pinball machines from all eras have been accumulated and housed in one little arena of American cool. You'll be amazed at the vast assortment of pin balls machines on display. It's a gamers paradise. For an endlessly fun way to spend an afternoon, you'll want to dedicate a few hours to this riveting selection of games.

For those who don't want to break the bank, over 50 games are free play meaning that you can play for only a small entrance fee. The sounds and the colours are enough to work you up into a whirl and this is a great place to take kids and introduce them a great American past time.

With two levels of pinball machines, you're spoilt for choice and nearly every pinball machine is equipped with a cup holder to place your bear – and that's the other thing, there are so many local beers to choose from to get your game going. When pinball machines meet beers the result is truly glorious. Game away your day at the hotly touted Pinball Museum. If you're not sure where to start, all machines lay out the aim of the game and offer fun little ratings to help you narrow down your search.

Visitor Tips: Stack up the quarters before your visit so you can play to your heart's content.

Green Lake Park

CC Image courtesy of iris on Flickr

Opening / Closing Times – 24h

Address / Contact Number: 5201 Green Lake Way N, Seattle, WA 98103, United States / 1 206-684-4077

Website –
http://www.seattle.gov/parks/park_detail.asp?id=307

Ticket Price – Can you buy in advance? Free entry
Average Visit Length? – 1-2h
Nearest car park –Roadside parking available
Nearest public transport stop – Metro, Woodlawn Ave Ne & Ne 71st St

Attraction Summary – Green Lake Park is a beautiful place to escape the city, should you be so inclined. Escape the urban sprawl for a moment and reconvene with nature. Open 24 hours, there's never a bad time to stop by. As one of Seattle's most loved parks, it's akin to New York's central park, an expanse of green and crystalline waters in the midst of the hubbub of day to day city life; a little jewel of tranquility that you can escape to any time. Thousands of locals and tourists alike are drawn to the city daily.

As a natural preserve, an endless array of plant and animal species as well as trees. The ideal spot for runners, walkers, skateboarders and roller bladders, the park has a 2.8 mile path surrounding the lake but it's also a great spot for boating, swimming and a romantic picnic.

The best time to visit is in spring and summer when temperatures are higher and the weather of Seattle can be enjoyed. The lake formed 50,000 years ago according to scientists and has been attracting visitors ever since. The perfect place to while away a lazy easy or get active, this park has something for everyone.

Visitor Tips: There's an indoor pool at Green Lake Park – one of just eight on Park lands.

Seattle Public Library

CC Image courtesy of Santhosh Rajangam on Flickr

Opening / Closing Times – 10am-8pm

Address / Contact Number –425 Harvard Ave E, Seattle, WA 98102, United States / 1 206-684-4715

Website – http://www.spl.org/

Ticket Price –Free entry

Average Visit Length? – 1hr

Nearest car park – Underground parking at the library, via Spring Street entrance, between 4th and 5th Ave.

Nearest public transport stop –5th ave

Attraction Summary – A library may not be your first port of call on vacation but this one is something special. The Seattle Public library is a phenomenal resource for the city attracting scholars, students, researchers and avid readers alike. The library houses over 2 million items for children, teenagers and adults including a range of books, music, movies, magazines and newspapers. Seattle city had been making efforts to start a communal library from as early as 1868 but the library finally came into being in 1890.

As the flagship Seattle library, the Seattle central library is an astonishing architectural feat comprised of 11 stories of glass and steel. The building has been voted as number 108 on the American Institute of Architects' 150 Favorite American structures. It's possible to take an architectural tour of the library exploring the tantalizing design that makes the library such a renowned landmark.

Unlike the conventional 'stuffy' library, Seattle's library is hugely inviting and also acts as a celebration of the survival of books in the technological driven digital age. The library was not conceived with a particular aesthetic in mind. Instead it was decided that the necessary functions of the library should dictate its appearance.

Visitor Tips: The library is a hub of cultural events from wine tasting to living history –if you prefer your reading without distractions, check the website calendar of upcoming events before your visit to miss the crowds.

Hiram M Chittenden Locks

CC Image courtesy of David Baron on Flickr

Opening / Closing Times – 10am-4pm

Address / Contact Number *–3015 NW 54th St, Seattle, WA 98107, United States / 1 206-783-7059*

Website – http://www.seattle.gov/tour/locks.htm

Ticket Price – N/A

Average Visit Length? – 2hr

Nearest car park –Car parking lot on site, street parking also available nearby.

Nearest public transport stop –54 stree

Attraction Summary – The Hiram M Chittenden locks are a complex array of locks that sit towards the west of Salmon Bay. Locals refer to them as the Ballard locks. The locks regulate the level of fresh water that enters Lake Washington and Lake Union and prevents saltwater intrusion. They also help boats adapt to the water levels of Puget Sound as they come in from the sea.

There are actually two locks and a range of fish present routinely use the Chittenden locks fish ladder for migratory purposes. There's also a range of gardens, sculptures, tourists and boats to take in making this a true feast for the eyes. It's best to visit the locks in-season to witness the fish jumping the fish ladder to spawn and a variety of boats transitioning between the locks.

The visitor center also helps you to learn more about the locks purpose and the array of native wildlife that flock there. If you're lucky, it may also be possible to catch sight of a seal! Catch a ranger talk to hear first hand information about how the locks operate.

There's no specific amount of time to spend at the locks; you might be lucky to see a lot in 5 minutes or choose to wait around to take in the atmosphere. Either way, it's part of a great day out.

Visitor Tips: Don't miss a visit to the botanical gardens when you come to the locks.

An in-season visit is advisable if you want to see the fish jumping

Pacific Northwest Ballet

CC Image courtesy of jwalsh on Flickr

Opening / Closing Times –

Address / Contact Number –*301 Mercer St, Seattle, WA 98109, United States*
/ 1 206-441-9411

Website – http://www.pnb.org/

Ticket Price –*Can you buy in advance?* Yes, ticket price varies.
Average Visit Length? 3h
Nearest car park – Seattle Centre, 650 3rd Ave North, Seattle, WA 98109

Nearest public transport stop **–Dexter Ave and Harrison**

Attraction Summary – The Pacific Northwest Ballet is a wonderful cultural experience for those who adore ballet troupes who embrace old classics such as the Nutcracker and Cinderella as well as mesmerizing modern dance collaborations. With helpful staff and reasonably priced tickets, it's relatively easy to get your culture fix in next to no time. You can catch an enchanting array of upcoming events including firm favorites and contemporary classics.

Based in Marion Oliver McCaw Hall, the relatively new space was unveiled in 2003 and provides a welcoming, hospitable space for this enthralling art form. As one of the most celebrated halls in the world, the space has helped Seattle root its ballet and opera talent. Whether you are a seasoned ticket holder or are in town to catch a show, the ballet always offers a wonderful day or night out with a touch of elitism and class.

Don't forget to try one of their cupcakes, complete with little plastic ballerinas! There are also a versatile range of food and drink options at intervals to keep yourself fed and watered throughout the performance and dance performances that work alongside the ballet to make sure that kids can follow allong with the story as it is told.

Visitor Tips: Tickets are snapped up quick. If you miss out and can't catch a performance while you're in town, the ballet also performs a limited touring schedule each year.

Museum of History and Industry

CC Image courtesy of Dana Flickr

Opening / Closing Times – 10am-5pm

Address / Contact Number – 860 Terry Ave N, Seattle WA, 98109 / 206-324-1126

Website – http://www.mohai.org/

Ticket Price – Can you buy in advance? Yes. Adults $17 Senior $15, Student $14, (under 14 free)
Average Visit Length? – 2hr
Nearest car park – AGC Lot, 1200 Westlake Avenue N, Seattle, WA 98109
Nearest public transport stop – Valley Street

Attraction Summary – No trip to Seattle is complete

without immersing yourself in the country's rich history and culture. Seattle's Museum of History and Industry offers a range of permanent and temporary exhibits designed to showcase Seattle's vibrant history.

Their three dimension collection consists of over 100,000 objects with a range of exhibitions that include local historical events, the 1962 World Fair, 1990 WTO riots, products invented and designed in the area, the artwork of local painters, and a range of clothing and textiles as well as everyday household items from Seattle's inception right through to the present day.

To get a taste of Seattle as it was and see how it has progressed through the years to become the city that you see today, the Museum of History and Industry is an absolute must.

If you're new to the area, either as a tourist or citizen, the museum offers a great way to really get to grips with the formation of the city and how it has changed and grown over the years. Highly educational but also endlessly fun, this trip is great for families as well as solo explorers who want to get to know Seattle beyond face value. The more you go, the more you'll see; this is one of those museums that will always surprise you.

Visitor Tips: The Museum is open late on Thursdays, with opening hours 10.00 am– 8pm.

Washington Baha'i History Museum

CC Image courtesy of Adib Roy Flickr

Opening / Closing Times – 11am - 3pm on T, W, S, Su.   Evenings: 7pm - 9pm on S, Su

Address / Contact Number –4341 1/2 University Way NE #210, Seattle, WA 98105

Website – http://bahaihistorymuseum-wa.org/

Ticket Price – *Can you buy in advance? No. A donation is requested.*

Average Visit Length? – 2h

Nearest car park – 4516 15th Ave NE , Seattle, WA 98105

Nearest public transport stop –University Way

Attraction Summary – The Washington Baha'i History Museum is a great place to go for a fusion of history artifacts that merge Washington's history with those of that Baha'i faith. Referred to as a boutique museum, the immaculate layout enables visitors to effortlessly explore in an utterly distinctive and entertaining way. This museum will make you think as it explores the tenants and ideals of the Christian faith alongside those of the Baha'i. As a non-profit museum, the focus is on bringing people from different communities, religions and backgrounds together to explore the hidden history of Seattle and to inspire.

The Baha'i faith arose in Persia in 1844 and was transmitted to Chicago during the Chicago World Fair. The museum explores some of the stories of the inhabitants who came over alongside their faith, utilizing pictures and artifacts to do so.

You can explore the museum freely or take a tour to find out more from an informed volunteer. Families can drop their kids off in the kids play area whilst they explore. As the museum is changed from time to time there is always more to see and learn and a lot can be taken away from this museum despite its relatively diminutive size.

Visitor tips: Entrance to the museum is free but a donation is requested by patrons. This goes towards the upkeep of the facility and its artifacts.

The museum runs several events each month including fireside conversations and question and answer sessions. If you have a particular interest in this area, check the web site calendar when planning your visit for upcoming dates for the diary.

Volunteer Park Conservatory

CC Image courtesy of VeloBusDriver Flickr

Opening / Closing Times – 10am-4pm

Address / Contact Number –1400 E Galer St, Seattle, WA 98112, United States / 1-206-684-4743

Website – http://www.volunteerparkconservatory.org/

Ticket Price – Can you buy in advance? Free entry (donation requested)

Average Visit Length? – 1hr

Nearest car park – Street parking is available

Nearest public transport stop – 15th Avenue East and East Galer Street

Attraction Summary – There's a lot going on at the Volunteer Park conservatory. The conservatory itself consists of 5 houses including the bromeliad house which houses over 2000 species and emphasises the plants colourful array of leaves.

The palm house consists of 1200 species including the oil, coco date and sago palm. The fern house consists of an array of exotic, tropical ferns whilst the seasonal display house is always flowering beautifully no matter what time of the year due to the changing floral displays. Finally, the cactus house consists of an assortment of cacti with their unusual, intriguing structures.

The garden's 45 acres were acquired in 1878 and is so named to honor those who dedicated their services during the Spanish-American war. As well as the conservatory, visitors can enjoy the Asian Art museum, water tower, and endless walking trails.

Although it's great to visit during spring and summer for the weather alone, there's really no wrong time to visit thanks to the seasonal displays. It's also the perfect way to brighten up a dowdy city day by surrounding yourself with highly colorful, fragrant exotic plants that really capture the senses. You can also catch some awesome views of the Space Needle from here so have your camera ready.

Visitor tips: If you're planning to visit with a group, tours are free on the first Thursday and Saturday of the month. Pre-booking is required.

Seattle Children's Theatre

CC Image courtesy of Seattle Municipal Archives Flickr

Opening / Closing Times – 9am-4pm

Address / Contact Number **–***201 Thomas St, Seattle, WA 98109, United States*
/ +1 206-441-3322

Website – https://www.sct.org/

Ticket Price – Can you buy in advance? Yes. Ticket prices vary.

Average Visit Length? – 3hr

Nearest car park – 1st Avenue North Garage: between John Street and Thomas Street, Seattle, WA 98109

Nearest public transport stop –Dexter Ave and Thomas St.

Attraction Summary – For those with little ones, Seattle is a city that knows how to please and the Seattle Children's Theatre is no exception. This is a great experience for children who love performance and extra meaningful for those that has never seen a play.

Although the shows are designed for children between the ages of 3 to 12, adults can also have a wonderful time. Introducing professional theatre to young audiences, a range of shows and events are on offer including Dick Whittington and his cat, Goodnight Moon and Robin Hood.

Celebrating 40 years of theatre, the Seattle Children's theatre also offers question and answer sessions following on from performances and offers a plethora of beginners' classes and advanced training sessions for kids who've caught the performance bug.

This is a truly inter-generational experience for all the family with parents, grandparents and kids enjoying a communal theatre experience that connects them.

The theatre orients the productions towards children with popular shows revamped with children and mind and shows specifically conceived for children. As such, there are many options for adults to indulge in too and many other fun things to partake in enabling you to spend a good few hours introducing your child to some culture.

Visitor tips: Booking recommended.

The Wing Luke Museum

CC Image courtesy of Nam-ho Park Flickr

Opening / Closing Times – 10am-5pm

Address / Contact Number *–719 S King St, Seattle, WA 98104, United States / +1 206-623-5124*

Website – http://www.wingluke.org/

Ticket Price *–14.95*

Average Visit Length? – 2hr

Nearest car park – Union Station Parking Garage, 401 S Jackson Street, Seattle, WA 98104

Nearest public transport stop –Chinatown-

International District Bus Tunnel Station

Attraction Summary – The Wing Luke Museum of the Asian Pacific American experience might sound like a mouthful but it is a must see. One of the museum's key selling points is its Bruce Lee museum – the only museum outside of Hong Kong dedicated to the legendary martial artist.

The museum introduces visitors to a range of tours and exhibitions designed to encapsulate the Asian experience of Pacific America offering an interesting cultural angle. Visitors are able to partake in a walking tour of Bruce Lee's Chinatown, retracing his footsteps and exploring some of his old haunts, including his first practice arena. Other options include a taste of China town to get your taste buds tingling, Touch of Chinatown which introduces newcomers to the smells and textures of Chinese ingredients, the Bitter and Sweet Tour and Historic Hotel Tour. Exhibitions include Bojagi, dedicated to Korean Americans, Art in Motion and In Struggle dedicated to Asian American acts of resistance.

There are also many portrait galleries to explore including I am Filipino, Vietnam in the Rear View Mirror and Our Roots Run Deep and Broad. To have a look at America through the eyes of Asian history, this museum is innovative, utterly unique and a must see.

Visitor Tips: The Museum is open late (until 8pm) on the first Thursday of each month.

The Museum organizes a number of tours including a historic downtown hotels tour and Chinatown – start at the museum and then head off with a guide.

Teatro ZinZanni

CC Image courtesy of Brad Coy Flickr

Opening / Closing Times – 6.30-10.30pm

Address / Contact Number –*222 Mercer St, Seattle, WA 98109, United States / +1 206-802-0015*

Website – http://www.zinzanni.com/seattle/

Ticket Price – Can you buy in advance? Yes, varies approx. $20+

Average Visit Length? – 3 hours

Nearest car park – Mercer Garage, 650 3rd Ave North, Seattle, WA 98109

Nearest public transport stop –King Street Station

Attraction Summary – Teatro ZinZanni is a great

option for those looking for something completely new. An alluring combo of part circus, part dinner theatre you can enjoy the entertainment whilst you dine. Perfect for large parties and group celebrations, this is a sure fire way to celebrate in style.

The show has been described as like the Kit Kat Klub but on acid...make of that what you will! For three unforgettable and utterly sensational hours, diners can enjoy a range of versatile performances incorporating international cirque, cabaret artists and comedy all under one roof.

With a range of only for the adults, family friendly shows, matinees and special celebrations, no matter when you are in town, there will be something on to your tastes. The round staging means there's no such thing as a bad seat and guests can dine on a range of appetizers, soups, salads, entrees and desserts in between acts including wild King Salmon and filet mignon.

With wine, cocktails and a plethora of alcoholic beverages flowing, you can enjoy the wild acrobatics from your seat but do be prepared for a little audience participation – the acts love dragging diners up on stage, particularly couples! Head down, eyes averted might not work in this show so be game for a laugh and go with the flow.

Visitor tips: The Teatro recommends bookings for dinner performances are made at least one week in advance. For weekends, booking two weeks in advance is advisable.

Klondike Gold Rush National Historical Park

CC Image courtesy of Tony Kent Flickr

Opening / Closing Times – 9-5pm

Address / Contact Number –319 2nd Ave S, Seattle, WA 98104, United States
/ +1 206-220-4240

Website – http://www.nps.gov/klse/index.htm

Ticket Price – Can you buy in advance? Free entry
Average Visit Length? – 1hr

Nearest car park – Mercer Garage, 650 3rd Ave North Seattle, WA 98109. Street parking is also available.

Nearest public transport stop – King Street Station, Pier 52 and Pier 50

Attraction Summary – Klondike Gold Rush National Historical Park is a must see stop on your trip to Seattle. Embracing one of America's last wild adventures, the Gold Rush has become something of legend. At the time, people all over America desperate to evade poverty went north, abandoning their responsibilities in the pursuit of gold. The trails, boomtowns and buildings that abounded during the Gold Rush era when men fled to find fortune.

This museum tells you all you need to know about those times with a range of trails and indoor and outdoor activities. The staff knows how to bring the experience to life transporting visitors back to the golden age itself and infusing the museum with grandeur.

The experience focuses on 5 particular individuals involved in the Gold rush in an informative and easily accessible way lending the legends a personal touch. The conditions, experiences and circumstances of each individual are readily on display and is completely free making it the perfect budget friendly choice for all. It's also a great place to take the family to learn a little more about Seattle's dynamic and exciting history. It might seem far flung now but it was once an everyday reality.

Visitor Tips: Special programs are often scheduled for the first Thursday of the month. Upcoming events are detailed on the website.

Keys on Main

CC Image courtesy of Tigist Sapphire Flickr

Opening / Closing Times – 7pm-2am

Address / Contact Number –11 Roy St, Seattle, WA 98109, United States /+1-206-270-4444

Website – http://keysonmain.com/seattle/

Ticket Price – Can you buy in advance? Yes, reservations accepted.

Average Visit Length? – 3 hours

Nearest car park – Mercer Street Garage, 650 3rd Ave North Seattle, WA 98109. Street parking is also available.

Nearest public transport stop –Dexter Ave N and Aloha St

Attraction Summary – Keys on Main dueling piano bar is a great experience for night time revelers looking for an unusual experience. The stage features two baby grand pianos and two performers. The two performers are selected from a versatile mix so no matter how many times you visit the show will be completely different in nature. Inspired by the audience, the crowd chooses what the performers play helping this become a show tailor made by you. It also means it's a totally once in a lifetime experience.

Group participation is enthusiastically encouraged with singing, cheering and general audience involvement going a long way towards the overall experience. The crowd drive the performance by selecting songs for them attached to a tip. The bigger the tip, the more likely the song is to be played.

For those that don't have the money on hand to go overboard, you can simply sit back and enjoy the direction in which the night is going. The versatile array of audience members ensures that no two songs are the same and that the vibe, genre, atmosphere and style are never consistent; always changing, always moving, always flowing – so you never get the same night twice.

Visitor tips: Audience participation is encouraged so don't be shy! The bar gets busy on weekends so arrive early for a good vantage point.

Golden Gardens Parks

CC Image courtesy of Wonderlane Flickr

Opening / Closing Times – 4am-11.30pm

Address / Contact Number *–8498 Seaview Pl NW, Seattle, WA 98117, United States*
+1 206-684-4075

Website –
http://www.seattle.gov/parks/park_detail.asp?ID=243

Ticket Price –Can you buy in advance? Free entry
Average Visit Length? – 3h
Nearest car park – Street parking by the beach
Nearest public transport stop –48 Ave SW and SW Findlay st

Attraction Summary – Gold by name, gold by nature, Golden Gardens park offers breathtaking views of Puget Sound as well as the Olympic Mountains. There's a lot going on with two wetlands, a looping walking trail, and a northern beach ideal for rugged hikes, leisurely strolls, sunbathing, swimming (if you can tolerate the cold) and fishing as well as watching boat launches from the bay.

Dog owners can also enjoy the gardens thanks to the off-leash dog area. The beach is mainly kept in tip top pristine condition thanks to its assortment of dedicated volunteers.

Developed by Harry W. Treat in 1907, the beach was envisioned as the perfect place for Seattle locals to take a sleepy Sunday off and get back to nature. Wonderfully communal, the beach is a popular spot for locals as well as in-town tourists and a great place to see the myriad of colorful characters that make up the city.

Naturally summer is the best time to visit where you can people watch and see all the swimmers, fishers, strollers and sports fans making the most of this stunning expanse. The park is home to endless fire pits enabling people to amble through and have a BBQ and is also home to plenty of ducks and turtles. Do you like volleyball? Be mindful that this is a prime spot!

Visitor Tips: Weekends in summer get busy so arrive early to get a parking spot. Don't forget to bring food and drink and stake your claim to a grill before lunch then cook up a storm and chill out for the rest of the afternoon.

Seattle Art Museum

CC Image courtesy of David Herrera Flickr

Opening / Closing Times – 10am-5pm

Address / Contact Number –1300 1st Ave, Seattle, WA 98101, United States / +1 206-654-3100

Website – http://www.seattleartmuseum.org/

Ticket Price – Can you buy in advance? Yes. Varies per exhibit

Average Visit Length? – 3 hours

Nearest car park – Russell Investment Centre Garage, 301 2nd Ave, Seattle, WA 98101

Nearest public transport stop –1st Ave and University Street

Attraction Summary – The Seattle Art Museum is a great place for art lovers to get their fix. If you fancy a little culture, head down for eye-popping art works. There are an endless array of collections and exhibits to pique all interests and tastes including the highly prestigious Pop Departures exhibit, American Art Masterworks for the patriotic and City Dwellers: Contemporary Art from India infused with all of the colour and crackle typically associated with Indian works.

There's also a riveting look at Indigenous beauty, Japanese Neo-Pop, and Northwest Coast Native Art that is quintessentially Seattle! Must see collections include African, American, Ancient American, Asian and Ancient Mediterranean collections as well as Aboriginal art, Islamic and European art works. With such an all-encompassing range, this museum can be enjoyed for hours as you take in all of the cultures, societies and art available.

With a constantly changing array of exhibitions, there is always something new to see and a range of programmes and learning opportunities. Informative, as you'd expect, this museum is also highly entertaining and truly catapults visitors across the globe traversing expanses such as culture, race and religion and piecing it all together into a cohesive whole. Ideal for a family trip or for a casual stroll through, make sure you keep a day spare for this one.

Visitor Tips: Photography is prohibited but sketching is permitted throughout the museum so be sure to bring ample paper, pencils, pastels or charcoal. The use of ink is not allowed.

Seattle Opera

CC Image courtesy of Bob B. Brown Flickr

Opening / Closing Times – depends on performance

Address / Contact Number –McCaw Hall, 321 Mercer Street, Seattle, WA 98109

Website – http://seattleopera.org/

Ticket Price –Can you buy in advance? Yes. Price depends on performance and location, from $ 77- $ 231
Average Visit Length? – 3h
Nearest car park – Mercer Street Garage, 650 3rd Ave North Seattle, WA 98109
Nearest public transport stop –Dexter ave n and Harrison st

Attraction Summary – Come to the Seattle Opera for

a true taste of class and culture in one of the world's most celebrated cities. Founded in 1963, the decadent, plush red staircase leading up to the opera entrance will remind you of the celebrity red carpet.

With 5 operas performed every year, there is enough of a selection for you to be spellbound by the heavenly ensemble of talented singers and performers. Theatrically compelling performances offer profound entertainment with an experience that elevates the senses.

Whether you're an opera veteran or you've never attended before, this is a must see occasion. The decadence of the hall still retains an easily accessible charm merging elitism with the every day. Even if you aren't the typical opera goer, you'll find yourself transfixed by this utterly magical experience.

Evening performances are the best, coupled with a nice dinner with loved ones and a chilled bottle of wine. A wonderful night out at the opera can easily be combined with dinner at the Space Needle or sunset views from one of the neighboring parks to complete the experience. A beautiful trip for couples or celebrations, if you have something special going on, take it to the opera.

Visitor Tips: Tickets are much in demand so plan your trip as far in advance as possible. A limited number of $25 tickets are available in the Second Tier Side Upper for every performance. Check the website for current availability.

Bruce Lee's grave, Lake View Cemetery

CC Image courtesy of Tony Fischer Flickr

Opening / Closing Times – 9.00am -8.00pm
(summer), 9.00am – 4.15 (winter)

Address / Contact Number –*1601 15th Ave E,
Seattle, WA 98112*, United States */+1* (206) 322-1582

Website
http://www.lakeviewcemeteryassociation.com/lees.php

Ticket Price – Can you buy in advance? Free entry
Average Visit Length? – 30 minutes
Nearest car park – Parking available at cemetery

Nearest public transport stop – *Grandview Pl E & E Garfield St*

Attraction Summary – A grave might not seem like an attraction high up on anyone's to do list but Bruce Lee's grave site has become something of a national treasure in the area. Located at Seattle's Lake View Cemetery, Bruce was renowned as a martial arts legend who made the move to movies and was much loved by Americans, his homeland Hong Kong and indeed by all.

He made a stir with his compelling, intricately woven martial arts moves. His grave attracts visitors from all over the world every day, many of whom leave flowers, coins and trinkets to honor the sacred resting place of this much loved star.

His scarlet red tomb stone is unmissable and is engraved with a photograph of Bruce himself. Positioned beside his son Brandon, the site has become something of a sacred pilgrimage for Bruce's legion of committed fans. It's a great place to sit and reflect on Bruce's success, fame and philosophies and also attracts many budding martial artists looking to pay respects to one of the first stars of the genre. Bruce is famous for breaching the boundaries between Asia and the Americas. Bruce died at the tragically young age of 32 but still remains a firm fixture in the minds of the American public.

Visitor Tips: The Cemetery closes at dusk each day so plan to visit earlier rather than later. It's close to Volunteer Park and Capitol Hill so make it the first stop of the day if time is short and you want to pack as much as possible in.

Smith Tower Chinese Room and Observation Deck

CC Image courtesy of ArtBrom Flickr

Opening / Closing Times – 10.00 am – 5.00 pm

Address / Contact Number – *506 Second Avenue, Ste. 220, Seattle, Washington 98104 /(206) 622-4004*

Website – http://smithtower.com/

Ticket Price – Can you buy in advance? No. Adults: $7.50 Students (w/ID): $6.00 Seniors (60+): $6.00 Children (6-12): $5.00 Children (5 & under): FREE

Average Visit Length? 30 mins
Nearest car park –500 2ND AV W, SEATTLE, WA 98119
Nearest public transport stop – Pioneer Square

Summary of attraction From less than glamorous beginnings on an old drug store lot, the Smith Tower Chinese Room and Observation Deck harks back to a golden era. The brain child of East Coast tycoon Lyman Cornelius Smith, his name sake building was once the tallest building in the West.

It no longer holds the lofty title but it has clung on to its past – the observatory and historic Chinese Room is a treasure trove of memorabilia from the turn of the Century with old newspapers on display with their centuries old headlines.

The Chinese Room itself is beautifully furnished, but even such treasures as the fabled Wishing Chair pale in comparison to the view. The Seattle skyline and its famous landmarks lie below – from the space needle and great wheel, International District and even Pioneer Square to Mother Nature's own contributions; Mount Rainieir and the Puget Sound, the Cascade and the Olympic Mountains. Whether you're interested in nature or industry, the 360 degree panoramic views mean you'll see just about everything Seattle is famous for. Tickets are on sale up to 20 minutes before closing time, which like a number of local attractions, changes according to the season.

Visitor Tips: The Observation Deck was designed with Seattle's notoriously damp weather in mind with great viewing points from both inside and outside so don't put off a visit if the weather isn't co-operating.

Last ticket sales for the Observation Deck are 20 mins before closing.

Burke-Gilman Trail

CC Image courtesy of Gene Bisbee Flickr

Opening / Closing Times – N/A

Address / Contact Number – Trail begins Seaview Av, Golden Gardens Park and ends 102nd Ave, Bothell / *(206)684-7583*

Website – http://www.seattle.gov/parks/BurkeGilman/bgtrail.htm

Ticket Price – Can you buy in advance? Free entry

Nearest car park – Street parking is available around the park along Golden Gardens Drive
Nearest public transport stop – Marymoor Park subway

Summary of attraction Snaking its way across the city from West to East, the Burke-Gilman Trail begins by Golden Gardens Park and threads its way to Bothell. At just shy of 19 miles long (officially the distance from start to end is 18.8 miles) it's quite a trek for the casual walker or tourist but a great length for those serious about cycling and hiking.

The great thing about the trail is it passes through or close by to lots of other top attractions so it can be combined with other activities and dipped in and out of without having to walk or bike the whole way. One of the forerunners of hiking trails in the country, it inspired others to follow suit and its easy to see why.

The trail begins in Golden Gate Park with a leisurely 2 mile stint and then is picked up again after Ballard Locks. Paved and safe, a stroll along the Trail will reveal such Seattle treasures as Gas Works Park, the University of Washington and the lake front.

If you tackle the entire trail, you'll finish at Bothell Park, having wandered by Log Boom Park. You can also sidetrack to the connected Sammamish River Trail.

Visitor Tips: The Burke- Gilman Trail is actually a busy commuter route as it passes through the University Campus and commercial centre. Avoid rush hour if you want a more leisurely stroll. You can also rent a bike en-route if you don't feel like walking.

Seattle Repertory Theatre

CC Image courtesy of Shannon Kringen Flickr

Opening / Closing Times – Address / Contact Number – 155 Mercer Street | PO Box 900923 | Seattle, WA 98109 / 206-443-2222

Website – http://www.seattlerep.org/

Ticket Price – Can you buy in advance? Yes. Tickets start at $15

Average Visit Length? 3 hours

Nearest car park – 170 MERCER ST, SEATTLE, WA 98109

Nearest public transport stop – Monorail, Seattle Center

Summary of attraction : For more than 50 years, the boards at the Seattle Repertory Theatre have been bringing much loved performances to life. The Theatre is celebrating its 50th anniversary with a star-studded artists council. Its luminaries include respected playwrights as well as Tony, Emmy and Oscar-nominated actors, giving some hint as to the well-class performances you can expect to see on stage.

With more than 500 productions to its name the Settle Repertory Theatre is as well known for its slick performances of popular plays as it is to its commitment for nurturing new talent. The Theatre is home to a thriving developmental program where writers and directors are able to hone their craft and bring exciting new works to life. It holds a regular New Play Festival making it the perfect destination for anyone passionate about the arts and keen to see the next big thing before it reaches cult, polished status.

There are a ton of local restaurants close to the theatre with pre-performance menus for those who want to dine beforehand. Seattle Repertory Theatre favorites include Agave, Peso's, Ten Mercer, The Melting Pot and The Sitting Room. There's a gift shop and snacks available inside.

Visitor Tips: If you're on a tight budget, try and catch a Wednesday matinee performance when tickets start from just $15.

There's major construction works going on around Mercer so expect delays if you're driving to the theatre.

Pre-order food from 9am on the day of the performance and collect when you arrive from the Espresso Stand.

The Center for Wooden Boats

CC Image courtesy of Dana Flickr

Opening / Closing Times – 10.00am -7.00pm

Address / Contact Number **–***1010 Valley St, Seattle, WA 98109, United States / +1 206-382-2628*

Website – http://cwb.org/

Ticket Price –Can you buy in advance? No. Boat rental $30 per hour (members), $35 per hour (non members)

Average Visit Length? – 2 hours

Nearest car park – North and South parking lots available on site.

Nearest public transport stop – Lake Union Park Street Car Stop

Attraction Summary – The quaint, idyllic and utterly picturesque Center for Wooden Boats is a postcard perfect sight so make sure you have your cameras at the ready. This is a very photogenic little spot! If you're used to the fabulous ferries dominating the waterfront then these disarmingly cute little boats make a welcome change.

This museum is a little different than others as all of the exhibits are outside and on the water making it a great outdoor experience and the perfect way to take in some fresh air.

The epitome of classic cool, these charming little wooden boats are well worth the visit. Staffed entirely by volunteers, it's well worth dropping by to support their project. Make sure to visit on a Sunday if you can to enjoy an old-fashioned boat trip with one of the skippers.

If you have sailing experience you can even take a boat out yourself so don't be afraid to ask. Even when the museum is closed it's still possible to catch a quick glimpse of the boats on the water. Be wary with little ones as not every area of the docks is child proofed. Exploring Seattle's boating history, complete with photographs and information is a great way to get closer to Seattle's seas.

Visitors Tips: If you want to be skippered, head to the Center on a Sunday for an old-fashioned boat trip. There's a free public sail all year round. Sign up from 10 am.

Best View Points in Seattle

The University of Washington

CC Image courtesy of Ming-yen Hsu Flickr

As one of America's most gorgeous campuses lined with beauteous blossom trees and verdant green lawns, from the university itself you can catch breathtaking views of the striking backdrop that is Mount Rainier, looming dominantly around the fair city. You can't catch the best view of downtown but there's a lot to photograph architecturally with the Suzzallo library nearby. Merging this cultured architecture with the striking natural beauty that abounds in Washington makes for some really intriguing and unusual shots that perfectly merge Seattle's wild, untamed natural expanses with clean, manmade structures. Be sure to stop by in spring to catch the blossom trees in full bloom.

How to get there: *Jump on Northwestern Trailways and walk the rest (it stops about 1 mile from campus) or get a Reliance Transport Shuttle from Spokane. The train and light rail can take you downtown where you can then transfer to one of 50 bus routes that service the university.*

Harbourview Park View Point

CC Image courtesy of Hollywata Flickr

If you want to snap some close up views in Seattle in all her glory, head to Harbourview. As it's such a close spot, you'll feel like you can legitimately reach out and touch the buildings before you. It's placed right in front of the medical center which is, of course, lit up like a Christmas tree at night. Seattle is awash with light and color at night transforming it into a brightly lit expanse that is profoundly photogenic. You can also see a lot of very close views of downtown Seattle and watch the cars duck and weave their way along the roads.

How to get there: *Take the 3, 4, 60, 205, 11, 211, 303, 941 or 942 bus.*

The Space Needle

CC Image courtesy of tdlucas5000 Flickr

Of course the Space Needle just had to be mentioned. It used to be Seattle's tallest landmark which makes it perfectly poised for that rotating 360 panorama of the city. From here, you can see it all; the mountains that serve as Seattle's backdrop, downtown, Pike Place Market and the ferries ebbing and bobbing on the water. Perhaps the only drawback is that as you're inside the Space Needle, you can't see this stunning and oh so utterly Seattle monument as well. This is by far one of the best ways to see the city and enables you to step inside a true Seattle staple.

How to get there: *Get to Broad Street (Seattle's most famous street) and turn left at the 4th Avenue and Broad Street intersection.*

Kerry Park

CC Image courtesy of Tiffany Von Arnim Flickr

Travelers flock to Kerry Park because it boasts one of the best views of the city. It remains the most popular viewpoint in Seattle and for good reason. Housed in a diminutive and utterly safe park, you can catch Seattle in its prime including the incredibly photogenic Space Needle.

Sunrise and sunset are popular times and you can easily line up your camera to fit in the entire city and watch the evening glow illuminate your photographs. Although it's a popular spot, it's not too crowded and you'll always manage to get your shots. Whilst you wait you can also catch ferries on their way in and out of the city.

How to get there: *Take metro route 1.*

Beacon Hill

CC Image courtesy of Wonderlane Flickr

Beacon Hill boasts beautiful views of the city. You can capture the Seahawks and Mariners stadiums in the same photo as that world famous sky line. It's a good place to come at dusk or sunset for that gorgeous glow that surrounds the city on a good day.

Here you'll be able to see the traffic from I-90 move onto the northbound I-5 which adds a little urban whirl to your photos as you capture busy citizens rushing in and out of the city. This, coupled with the stillness of the architecture makes for a really riveting shot. Early morning is also a good time to pop down and take a photo to watch the city wake up.

> ***How to get there****: Get the Link Light Rail to Beacon Hill station.*

Alki Beach

CC Image courtesy of Nick Bramhall on Flickr

Alki Beach boasts breathtaking views of the water. You can catch the ferries coming in and out and also take in the spectacular sight of the Ferris wheel which dominates pictures and enthuses them with a sense of fun and play.

It's a great place to come in summer when the beach is packed with swimmers, sunbathers and sports fans. Volleyball is particularly popular here! You can catch some very communal snaps that bring Seattle to life. There are also some great views of the city from here and some stunning architecture and statues that really breathe life into the city.

> **How to get there**: Take the King County water taxi from Pier 50.

Belvedere View Point

CC Image courtesy of Atomic Taco Flickr

This park is renowned for its gorgeous views of Elliot Bay and downtown Seattle. On good days, you can see right across to the Cascade Mountains and Mt Rainier. It's a popular destination for weddings and ceremonies and there are plenty of photo opportunities here.

Many claim that it is the best view of Seattle also catching the water and ferries that traverse it for an all-encompassing sight that showcases the very best of Seattle. It's also a popular spot for couples because of the romance of the location. It's a small park but the views it offers are big.

How to get there: *Get a bus to admiral way.*

Gas Works Park

CC Image courtesy of Wildcat Dunny Flickr

This park has it all. You can catch Seattle's striking skyline, rolling lush hills and even abandoned industrial gas works for stunning photo ops. Famous for its 4th July Fireworks displays, you can take an endless plethora of photos capturing the cityscape with the verdant grass that grows in abundance. Photos taken here have a real 'city meets nature' feel which makes for some interesting combinations. For those of you who'd rather see than snap, it's a great opportunity to look in on the city from a distance and gain a little peace and tranquility before you return to the madness.

> ***How to get there***: Head to stop 26920 on Wallingford Ave

Seattle Great Wheel

CC Image courtesy of Grant Montgomery Flickr

Jump on the Seattle Great wheel to see a truly interesting view of Seattle. As one of Seattle's most historical landscapes situated just beside Waterfront Park, you can catch a high up view of the city that is hard to beat. To add a little comfort, opt for a VIP chair and seat yourself on plush leather with a glass bottom that shows you what's beneath your feet. The views from here are a little different to any you'll see anywhere else purely because you'll be in motion! You'll get to see beaches, mountains, water and the city. Afterwards head to Waterfront Park to catch the same views from the ground.

> **How to get there**: *Number 4 bus to downtown Seattle*

The Sky View Observatory

CC Image courtesy of Joe Wolf Flickr

As the tallest building in Seattle the Sky View observatory does exactly what it says on the tin. With an all-encompassing 360 panoramic view, you really can't go any higher, unless you opt for a balloon ride.

You can see it all; Elliot Bay, the mountains that frame the city, the Space Needle, the ferries on the water and jaw dropping views of the city itself. It's a great place to come if you're only in the city for a short time to make sure that you get to see everything that you want to see in the best way possible.

How to get there: *Number 12 bus*

Best Day Trips From Seattle

Mount Rainer National Park

CC Image courtesy of Jon Dawson Flickr

Opening / Closing Times – na

Address / Contact Number – 39000 State Route 706 E, Ashford, WA 98304

1-360-569-2211

Website – http://www.nps.gov/mora/index.htm

Ticket Price – Vehicle: $15
Individual: (on foot, bicycle, motorcycle) $5. Children 15 years old and younger are admitted free of charge.

Average Visit Length? –6 hours

Nearest car park – Car parking available at visitor centres

Nearest public transport stop –N / A *(national park shuttle service not available due to budget restrictions)

Attraction Summary – Take a trip to Mt Rainier – an active volcano and beautiful National Park. Seattle is renowned the world over for its marvelous mountainous ranges and the scenery is beyond picturesque and idyllic. Mt Rainier is perhaps the most dramatic of all so if you're going to pick just one mountain to see up close, make it this the one. The mountain has a lush grace and stunning natural fauna highlighting the bold juggernaut in the background. Although you can spy the mountain from downtown, it's so much more impressive to see its magnificence close up. You'll most certainly be impressed by its swopping grandeur. You also get to explore wildflower meadows, amazing waterfalls and traditional untouched forests. With a peak that stands over 14,000 feet tall, you can enjoy being up close and personal rather than far away and you'll have a newfound appreciation of the mountain when you get back to the city. Whatever you do, do not forget your camera as such intimate views might not be able to be replicated. Expert guards are on hand to tell you all you need to know so you can learn as you go. It's also a great chance to escape the city for a short while.

Visitor Tips: Snow in winter means some of the park is inaccessible so check the website and weather updates before travelling if you plan to go outside of peak season.

Tilicum Village Cultural Experience

CC Image courtesy of Rick Moerloos Flickr

Opening / Closing Times – N/A

Address / Contact Number – Lake Island, Seattle, WA 98126, Tel: 206-623-1445 Ticket **Price** – Can you buy in advance? – Yes, several tour operators run trips to the Village including Argosy Cruises and Viator

Average Visit Length? – **4 hr**

Nearest car park – Ferries depart Pier 55

Attraction Summary – The Tilicum Village Cultural Experience is located a mere 8 miles from Seattle's waterfront on Blake Island State Park. If you're intrigued to learn more about the indigenous Native American's who traversed the land, this place offers interesting insights into their culture, artwork and way of life as well as having the opportunity to witness the performance of traditional song and dance routines.

There's also a delicious buffet to keep you full during proceedings. The ferry ride over is superb enough with gorgeous views of Seattle behind and of course, the superb sea below you.

Once you arrive, you get to see the longhouse itself and are free to enjoy a tasty appetizer of clams and nectar. Acquaint yourself with the myths and legends of the Native peoples with the cultural heritage showcased via performance, theatrics, symbolism and captivating storytelling.

You can also enjoy the beach and trails that abound on the island before returning to the city, which might seem a little less magical in comparison after such a trip! Learning about the ancestry of the Native people is a really enriching, exciting and informative process brought to life at Tilicum Village. Make sure you don't miss this one.

Visitor Tips: Bring comfy walking shoes or sneakers as you'll want to explore the grounds to see the deer and other wildlife.

Victoria, British Columbia

CC Image courtesy of LASZLO ILYES Flickr

Opening / Closing Times – na

Web Address http://www.tourismvictoria.com/

Ticket Price – Can you buy in advance? –N/A
Average Visit Length? NA
Nearest car park –na
Nearest public transport stop – NA

Attraction Summary – Take a trip to Victoria, British Columbia from Seattle for the perfect day trip. A charming destination where new meets old, Victoria is an island that you'll spend hours exploring. It is packed with architecture, quaint old shops, inviting tea rooms and breath taking vistas. Spend the day exploring on foot, all the better to discover tempting nooks to sample a craft beer, piping hot coffee or cheeky cocktail as the sun goes down.

The island itself offers the adventurous visitor lots to do, and the challenge may be packing your entire to do list into just one day. There are an abundance of parks and a choice of outdoor activities to sample from kayaking and hiking to cycling and even zip lining.

Exploring on two wheels is a great way to see more of what Victoria has to offer and will mean you cove r a greater distance than would be possible on two feet.

If you plan to do some shopping, head to Government Street to pick up a few souvenirs or Trounce Alley, a local secret, to browse European fashions. To refresh after your retail exertions, a few short steps to Bastion Square will present a choice of restaurants as well as handmade crafts and a market in summer.

Visitor Tips: Vicitoria is a great place to shop for antiques and hand made products. Look out for local crafts around Bastion Square. Don't leave without stopping to sample afternoon tea or savor a craft beer which Victoria is becoming known for.

Olympic National Park

CC Image courtesy of Frank Kovalchek Flickr

Opening / Closing Times – na

Address / Contact Number : Olympic National Park Visitor Center, 3002 Mount Angeles Road, Port Angeles, WA 98362. 1-800-833-6388

Website – http://www.nps.gov/olym/index.htm

Ticket Price: Vehicle: $15
Individual: (on foot, bicycle, motorcycle) $5. Children 15 years old and younger are admitted free of charge.
Average Visit Length? N/A
Nearest car park – N/A
Nearest public transport stop –The Washington State Ferry System serves a number of routes within the area as does the Clallam Transit System.

Attraction Summary –
Fancy getting out of the city and into the wild unknown? The Olympic National Park is close to one million acres

and three parks in one. It is a stunning option when you want to get out of the city and up close with Mother Nature. Housing some of America's oldest forests, the Park is beautiful in summer and in winter- just don't forget your snow shoes!

There's a lot going on here with serene beaches, old forests fresh out of a fairy tale and looming mountains serving as the perfect backdrop. A truly marvelous ecosystem native to the Park has also seen the evolution of sixteen plant and animal species that exist nowhere else in the world. This makes a day trip a unique experience for animal lovers and botanists.

Hurricane Ridge is well worth looking out for which takes you to the very brink of the park's jagged peaks for breathtaking views. There are a lot of options to spot wildlife including marmots and black-tailed deer to help your pictures brim with life.

If you need a little fresh air away from the city, this park is an absolutely enchanting exploration where you'll get to see rugged wilderness and raw beauty up close and personal.

Visitor Tips: Expect heavy traffic in summer which can significantly add to your journey time.

If you plan to camp, there is no pre-booking of camp sites at most of locations with pitches first come, first served. You can make reservations at Kalaloch campground during the summer months.

Snoqualmie Falls

CC Image courtesy of Kunal Mukherjee Flickr

Opening / Closing Times – na

Address / Contact Number – **6501 Railroad Ave SE Snoqualmie, Washington, 98024**
Website – http://www.snoqualmiefalls.com/

Ticket Price – Can you buy in advance? – NA
Average Visit Length? 2- 3hrs
Nearest car park –There is free parking at the entrance to the falls
Nearest public transport stop Railroad Ave S & SE King St

Attraction Summary –

Wine and waterfalls make an appealing mix and a day trip to Snoqualmie Falls complete with a Seattle winery tour is ideal if you're looking for a day trip to take you out of the city for a little while. Explore foothills, beautiful flower farms and exciting all-American horse ranches. As with most of Seattle, a fair few movies have been shot here including the Vanishing and Twin Peaks so you might recognize a few familiar sights. Such a trip is ideal for those who want to explore the stunning waterfalls and be at one with nature whilst also indulging in the finer things in life.

The waterfalls as the piece de resistance are utterly quaint and idyllic and the perfect escape from the city. Whether you book a tour with a trustworthy company or take a trip yourself, it's a good idea to head here especially if you want to catch the real wild side of Seattle up close and personal with a few treats to hand.

Snoqualmie Falls are one of Washington State's most visited attractions so it's wise to plan your visit in advance, especially if you plan to stay overnight at one of the local guest houses or lodges.

Visitor Tips: Book on to a tour to couple a trip to the falls with a vineyard visit. This is especially worth doing in summer when thousands of tourists flood into the area, making it one of the most visited attractions in the state.

Mount St Helens

CC Image courtesy of skedonk Flickr

Opening / Closing Times – na

Address / Contact Number – Johnston Ridge Observatory, 24000 Spirit Lake Highway, P.O. Box 326 Toutle, WA 98649 (360) 274-2140

Mount St. Helens National Volcanic Monument Headquarters, 44218 NE Yale Bridge Road, Amboy, WA 98601, (360) 449-7800

Website – http://www.fs.usda.gov/mountsthelens

Ticket Price – Can you buy in advance? Day pass, $5 can be ordered online.

Average Visit Length? –6 hr
Nearest car park –na
Nearest public transport stop –na

Attraction Summary –

Seattle is backed by an endless plethora of breathtaking mountains and stunning picturesque views so getting out of the city to see them close up is a must when in town. If you are hard pressed for time, pick a mountain and stick with that. St Helen's is an interesting choice because it houses a presently dormant volcano. Don't miss a visit to the Johnson Ridge Observatory to discover gorgeously panoramic views of the Mount St Helens National Volcanic Monument and to discover all you could ever need to know about the 1980 eruption. As one of the most disparaging eruptions in the history of America, it's very interesting to learn about the destruction and chaos that resulted. There are also plenty of nature walks and short hikes so it's important to bring comfortable attire.

Spring or summer is the best seasons to visit so that you can enjoy a picnic in the striking wilds. You can also follow the eruption trail to see the path of the volcano itself and to view the phenomenal lava dome, crater and the landslide deposit area. To get so up and close to a volcano is an absolutely once in a lifetime experience with endless unique photo opportunities.

Visitor Tips: Try and visit in spring or summer to get the most out of your time in the Park.

iFLY Seattle

CC Image courtesy of Loren Javier Flickr

Opening / Closing Times – 11am-11pm

Address / Contact Number – 349 Tukwila Pkwy, Tukwila, WA 98188, United States

Phone:+1 206-244-4359

Website –https://seattle.iflyworld.com/

Ticket Price – Can you buy in advance? –yes, varies $59.95

Average Visit Length? –2 hr

Nearest car park –Tukwila

Nearest public transport stop –Andover Park

Attraction Summary –

If you fancy getting out of Seattle and doing something beyond the ordinary, iFLY Seattle is a great way to test your metal. An exciting alternative to outdoor skydiving, the indoor skydive experience takes place entirely inside but compromises on none of the thrill, adrenaline and boldness!

Whether you'd never want to do an actual skydive but want to experience the rush or just want to see what it's all about before you commit to the big jump, iFLY Seattle gives daredevils the opportunity to feel like they're flying.

Recreating real free fall conditions, you'll experience all of the awe of skydiving without having to jump out of a plane. The vertical wind tunnel flushes out speeds of up to 160mph which surrounds you with a roomful of air on which you are able to float, suspended. It doesn't require a pesky parachute or any freefall dives – and it offers people one of the most exhilarating adrenaline rushes of their lives.

The experience is great for everyone, including children and those with disabilities although shoulder and neck injuries can cause exemptions. If you fancy getting out of the city for a couple of hours and and doing something different, this experience is well worth considering.

Visitor Tips: If you can go on a weekday, do so as it gets much busier on weekends.

Adventure Paintball Park

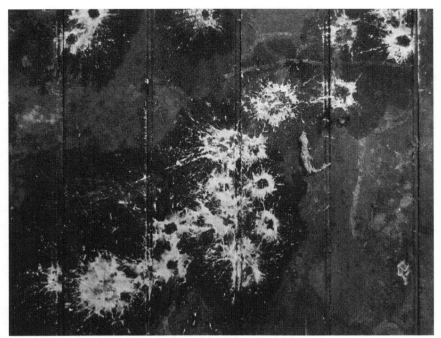

CC Image courtesy of Paul Gallo Flickr

Opening / Closing Times – WALK ON PLAYERS - ONLY
Saturdays 1:00 PM -5:00 PM, otherwise you need to
prebook
Address / Contact Number –6357 Whiteman Road KP
S. Longbranch, WA 98351

Contact Number (253) 793-7000

Website –http://www.adventurepaintballpark.com

Ticket Price – Can you buy in advance? –yes for
parties, walk on rate $55 each player
Average Visit Length? –3hr

Nearest car park – at the centre
Nearest public transport stop –na

Attraction Summary –

Seattle is not quite as serene as it might have you thinking it is on the surface. If you fancy getting dirty, you only need to travel 90 minutes out of the city to find the Adventure Paintball Park.

You can spontaneously turn up for one of their Saturday walk-on sessions or you can book your own private party and cultivate your own ideal paintball scenario with an option frighteningly entitled, 'Most Dangerous Game.'

This is an option for all those who love a little bit of an adrenaline rush. It's also a great way to have a memorable experience with your travel gang and get out of the city for a little while to see what delights exist beyond the city centre.

This is one of those true hidden gems nestled just outside of the city that offers hours of fun. It can be as calm or as frightening as you want it to be. You can tailor make your game to just the right amount of risk.

If you have kids why not take them to the child-friendly kids paintballing parties? Fully qualified instructors guide play so that nothing gets out of hand. This is a delightfully adventurous way to spend a Saturday.

Visitor tips: Advance booking required

Hibulb Cultural Center and Natural History Preserve

CC Image courtesy of Blake Handley Flickr

Opening / Closing Times – 10am-5pm

Address / Contact Number –

Hibulb Cultural Center and Natural History Preserve
6410 23rd Avenue NE Tulalip, Washington 98271
info@HibulbCulturalCenter.org
FAX: 360.716.0826

Website –http://www.hibulbculturalcenter.org/

Ticket Price – Can you buy in advance? –$10.00 per adult
Average Visit Length? –2hr
Nearest car park –at the centre

**Nearest public transport stop –
Everett Amtrak**

Attraction Summary –

The Hibulb Cultural Centre is a great way to immerse yourself in the indigenous culture of the Native American Tulalip Tribes. The centre's mission is to preserve, protect, collect, enhance and share the history, values and fascinating beliefs of the various Tulalip Tribes. As successors to various other tribes including the Snoqualmie, Skykomish and Snohomish, the centre consists of 23,000 square feet and 50 acres of cultural insights. It's also fully interactive, enabling you to take a hands on approach to the experience. You can peruse maps etched in painstakingly intricate detail which depict the various bloodlines of the tribes, see a longhouse and share in the legends and myths which abound in this most magical of cultures.

It's a great way to find out much more about the history, culture, symbolism and stories of the tribes and you can spend hours enmeshing yourself in this enriching experience. Located not far from the city, it makes the perfect day trip for those looking to explore and unearth some intriguing secrets. The Native American's remain an enchanting group of people with a very rich and dynamic history. Finding out more about them is essential whilst you are out of town. There are many exhibits and collections which showcase artefacts, tools, equipment, items and artwork belonging to the tribes.

Visitor tips: The entrance fee is waived on the first Thursday of every month

Maury Island

Opening / Closing Times – na

Address / Contact Number –na
Website –
http://www.kingcounty.gov/recreation/parks/naturalreso
urces/naturallands/mauryislandsite.aspx

Ticket Price – Can you buy in advance? – free, just
price of ferry
Average Visit Length? –2hr
Nearest car park –no parking on site
Nearest public transport stop – ferry stop

Attraction Summary –

UFO lovers will just adore this next stop. Maury Island is a mere 70 minutes south and will transport you to a world of conspiracy. Back in June of 1947, Maury Island was visited by flying saucers or so the legends say. There is of course absolutely no way to prove this rumour but visiting the island for yourself is a great way to see if you can unearth your own clues.

Many say that the island is cloaked in an eerie calm with intriguing staples such as the protruding lighthouse located at Point Robinson Park and the craggy, rugged mile-long shore that looks like something straight out of space. Whether you believe in the conspiracy theories or just fancy an adventure, it's a cool little island to explore and a great way to get further afield from the city to find out a little more about the myths and legends that surround the shores.

Earlier in 2014, a documentary was made about the Maury Island UFO incident weighing up the possibility of truth with the potential that it was a hoax. Whatever side of the fence you sit on, it's still a very interesting place to come and see for yourself.

Visitor tips: This area is relatively unspoilt and no cars or motorized vehicles are allowed on the island so comfortable walking shoes are a must.

Shopping / Markets in Seattle

Pike Place Market

CC Image courtesy of Theodore Scott Flickr

Pike Place market is Seattle's oldest and you can do it all here. There are endless restaurants to grab a feed including plentiful bowls of piping hot chowder.

Seattle is known for its seafood so make sure you sample some. As well as restaurants, you can look at crafts, local produce and people watch. The markets are always heaving and are free to enter.

You can spend a whole day simply wandering around and it's a place where the air is thick with excitement. There's a reason why this market has endured for so long – it's fun, engaging and got everything that you need.

How to get there: Grab the metro or transit light rail to first avenue or Pine street.

University Village

CC Image courtesy of spaetz Flickr

University Village is one of Seattle's prime shopping spots. There's an endless array of shops, dining experiences and events on making this the ideal place to head on a weekend to pick up a few souvenirs or holiday treats. Clean, spacious and well maintained, you can find University Village a little far north of downtown Seattle. There are plenty of well-known local and international brands as well as ample little boutiques to support. Whether you're a window shopper or have something particular in mind, this is a fun little place to spend some time and attracts a wide range of locals and tourists.

How to get there: Take route 32, 43, 68 or 75 on the bus.

Ballard Farmer's Market

CC Image courtesy of Valerie Hinojosa Flickr

For fresh, organic, in season and local produce head to Ballard Farmer's Market. Here the locals get their merchandise out to display a teaming smorgasbord of color and heady aromas. This hugely popular spot is a mainstay for locals who shop for their ingredients here.

Ideal if you have something healthful and nutritious in mind, you'll also be supporting local trade. Veggies, fruits, prime cuts of meat and of course plenty of seafood (Seattle's staple) abound here meaning that whatever's on the menu you can pick up an affordable array of scrumptious addictions to add flare and fire to your food.

How to get there: Take the number 3 downtown.

Uwajimaya

CC Image courtesy of Nicholas Wang Flickr

If you're in Chinatown, you need to head to Uwajimaya. It's Chinatown's number one supermarket and is full of delicious Chinese staples. The Asian influence in this area is strong and the tasty exotic fare is perfect if you're throwing together a far flung dinner. This is also a place to find those obscure Asian ingredients that can't be found elsewhere making it ideal for Seattle's Korean, Japanese, Vietnamese, Chinese and Filipino citizens but also for those with a preference towards Asian eats. It's the equivalent of an Asian food Disneyland with every ingredient you could ever dream of housed inside.

How to get there: Bus 3 to downtown, then take the 102 bus to Fairwood.

Westfield Southcentre

CC Image courtesy of Joe Wolf Flickr

Fancy a Saturday shop? The Southcentre Westfield consists of your typical international, global shopping staples and plenty of local little boutiques. You'll find all your big brands here and also some lesser known stores. With a plethora of restaurants, stores, food courts and events, there's enough to do here to keep everybody entertained for hours. It's immaculately clean and also attracts plenty of visitors in droves looking to acquire a few items. It's the type of center you enter expecting to stay for one hour and don't end up leaving for five more. A hotspot for locals, plenty of tourists venture out here too.

> *How to get there: Number 3 bus downtown; bus 4 to Judkins Park; walk to Pioneer Square; 150 Bus towards Kent*

Bella Umbrella

CC Image courtesy of tour geek Flickr

Seattle is a city of extremes. On a pleasant day, the weather can be absolutely gorgeous but catch it during a bad one, and you'll wish you'd brought an umbrella! Bella umbrella consists of a range of lovingly rendered handmade umbrellas in a range of stunning, utterly spellbinding colors. Popular with the locals, you'll see many a Bella Umbrella erected in the rain and you'd be well placed to follow suit. Bright, bold and beautiful and available in many styles and patterns, you'll never have known that umbrellas could be so stylish and fashionable. Bella means beautiful and that's what these brollies are.

How to get there: Walk to Wall Street from the Space Needle. E line bus towards downtown. Walk to 1st Avenue

Seattle Mystery Bookshop

CC Image courtesy of Denise Krebs Flickr

Avid readers should shoot to Seattle's mystery bookshop. Whether you know what you're looking for or don't have a clue, this bookshop is located downtown and offers a range of favorites and contemporary classics from the mystery genre. This bookshop stocks a range of books from authors who are not always easy to find making it a great place to pick up an engaging new read. As an independent bookstore, the selection is huge making this the perfect playground for those who love their tomes. The staff is also able to get their hands on any book you require. All you need do is ask.

> *How to get there: bus 4 downtown; 3 bus towards Madrona*

Magic Mouse

CC Image courtesy of Ruthanne Reid Flickr

Magic Mouse is one of Seattle's greatest authentic toy stores stocking every kind of game, toy and plaything imaginable. It's a giant playground for kids and big kids alike and the perfect place to pick up a birthday or Christmas gift or any other for a special occasion. Whether you're looking for games, puzzles, stuffed animals, kites, models, books, puppets or more you can find it here and half of the fun is looking. The shelves are brimming with interesting and appealing merchandise. Unlike commercial toy stores, the toys stocked here are more authentic and one of a kind harking back to a rose tinted nostalgic past where children played with more bespoke, unique pieces.

How to get there: 4 bus downtown; 3 bus towards Madrona

Pacific Place

CC Image courtesy of Jason Burrows Flickr

This indoor mall has it all; shops, restaurants and a cinema. Located on Pine Street, nearby Pike Place Market you can combine two trips in one day. The mall is gorgeously decorated with cutting edge contemporary style in mind. The brands here are a little high end but if you have the cash to spend, you can pick up a luxurious present for yourself. The welcome desk caters to shoppers and lost tourists alike so you'll find many people wandering in and out at all times. Stores include L'Occitaine, Victoria's Secret and Tiffany's. There are many mid-to-high range outlets here to treat yourself to a little something special.

How to get there: 4 bus downtown; walk to 6th Avenue

Archie McPhee

Image courtesy of Bjørn Giesenbauer Flickr

If you're looking for something weird, whacky or wonderful, head to Archie McPhee. Amongst the surreal selection include such eccentricities as foie gras flavored bubble gum, two headed baby dolls, Jesus action figures, rubber chickens, magic 8 balls and bacon bandages. This is the store for the ideal gag gift and is fun just to look around. Most find the store by accident and through word of mouth it's become quite the phenomenon. If you're searching for presents for parties, Halloween costume adornments or bachelor party jokes, Archie's is the place to head to. Other items include classic pin-up photos, snow globes, bacon toothpaste, the world's largest underpants and fake limbs.

How to get there: E line bus towards Aurora village

Activities in and around Seattle

Savour Seattle Food Tours

Opening / Closing Times – 9am-5pm

Address / Contact Number –_1916 Pike Place, Suite 12-480, Seattle, WA 98101 /206-209-5485

Website –http://www.savorseattletours.com/

Ticket Price/Can you buy in advance? – Yes - Average Visit Length? –2-3 hours
Nearest car park (address with post code) – Pike Place Market Parking - 98101
Nearest public transport stop –Pine Street

Attraction Summary – Combining culinary delights with an on foot tour of Seattle city is the perfect way to explore. Having featured in various publications including Frommer's Travel Guide and USA Today, visitors can enjoy a range of award-winning eats and elitist wines on a tasting tour that fuses culture and history with taste.

Seattle is known as one of the world's most prestigious culinary destinations with a plethora of scrumptious seafood, winning wines and decadent chocolates for those who wish to indulge their sweet tooth. One of the most engaging aspects of the tour is that the friendly and knowledgeable guides never revert to a script. Instead they allow the info and humor to flow as their expertise of the city shines through and enthuses their preparation. Options include the 'Booze n' Bites' which merges wonderfully wines with bite sized delicacies for a short and sweet sample to further tantalize your taste buds and the 'VIP Market Tour' which takes travelers into the heart of Seattle's historical Pike Place Market. Such tours enable you to see the market the way it was meant to be seen; experienced firsthand as a complete sensory experience of taste, touch, smell, sight and sound in the company of fellow travelers.

Visitor Tips:

- Beware – food comas are probable! Pace yourself to avoid getting too full or drunk too soon. There's a lot to sample!
- Chocolate Lovers should cement their spot on the 'Chocolate Indulgence Tour' to sample Seattle's sweet side.

Seattle Wine Tours

Opening / Closing Times – 9am-5pm
Address / Contact Number –4660 East Marginal Way, Seattle, WA 98104 / 206-444-9463

Website –http://www.seattlewinetours.com/

Ticket Price/Can you buy in advance? –Yes - $114.25
Average Visit Length? – 3 hours
Nearest car park (address with post code) – EZ Airport Parking 10817
Nearest public transport stop –S Clovedale St & 12th Ave St

Attraction Summary – Seattle is known for three things; it's views, it's seafood and its wine. An ideal way to sample a range of delicious wines is to book yourself on a tour. Ideal for small, medium or large sized groups, visitors get to experience a range of tantalizing tastes and bottled delicacies. With an extensive range of highly qualified, knowledgeable staff who understands how to merge a patient, informative and entertaining approach to keep guests intrigued, no two tours are quite the same.

Such tours are ideal for families, friends and co-workers and are perfect for celebratory events. Tourists in town can enjoy a range of Washington wines and take in the beautifully scenic surroundings and is ideal for a completely special and unique experience. Taking in the splendid natural beauty of Seattle whilst enjoying an array of alcoholic beverages is the perfect way to learn more about the culture, history and geography of this breathtaking area whilst also enjoying tailor made tastes specific to each visitors alcohol specifications.

Ideal for tourists and also those local to the area who want to see Seattle from an entirely new side. Visitors are able to visit a plethora of wineries to gain a versatile, tempting taste of the city.

Visitor Tips:

- If you aren't a wine buff, feel free to mention your preferences to your tour guide. They may be able to fit you in a few other alcoholic beverages

Paris Eastside Cooking Class

Opening / Closing Times – 9am-5pm

Address / Contact Number –_816 east Pike, Seattle, WA 98122 / 2064523622

Website – http://www.pariseastside.com

Ticket Price Can you buy in advance? –Yes - $40-$60
Average Visit Length? – 3 hours
Nearest car park (address with post code) - Pike Place Market Parking - 98101
Nearest public transport stop – Pine Street

Attraction Summary – Seattle is world renowned for its delicious delicacies, in particular the sea food that abounds in the surrounding seas. Although the city flourishes with restaurants, cafes and eateries, participating in a cooking class is a great way to immediately boost your culinary repertoire. As the name suggests, the Paris Eastside Cooking class focuses on all things French including wines, chocolates and a range of meats.

As the foodie capital of the world, everything Paris is evoked in this charming little cookery class, enabling guests to put their chopping, grilling and sautéing skills to the test. Lead by experts in French cooking, chefs can prepare artful plates under the watchful tutelage of experienced staff who offer handy hints and time tested tips.

The classes appeal to couples looking to cook up a romance enthused meal for one another, families and groups of friends looking to do something different. For those looking to expand their cooking skills learning the foundations as well as the intricacies of French cuisine is an absolutely essential way to immediately amp up your kitchen talents in an enduring, lifelong manner. The best thing is that you get to eat what you've made. The proof is in the pudding so they say.

Visitor Tips:

- Dreary day? Head to a cooking class during the autumn and winter seasons for an exciting indoor endeavor
- Have a sweet tooth? Make macaroons

Seattle Free Walking Tours

Opening / Closing Times – 9am-5pm

Address / Contact Number –_2000 Western Ave, Seattle, WA 98101 / +1 360-201-5611

Website – http://seattlefreewalkingtours.org/

Ticket Price - Can you buy in advance? –No – Pay what you feel

Average Visit Length? – 3 hours

Nearest car park (address with post code) – Market Place Garage, 98121

Nearest public transport stop –Pine Street

Attraction Summary – Exploring the city by foot is absolutely essential. Seattle is spellbinding from every angle; water, air and viewpoint but strolling through the city on foot definitely immerses you in the action firsthand. The entertaining and informative guides will fill you in on the culture, history and geography of the city as you wander helping to educate you in an exciting way.

There are a variety of walking tours on offer completely dependent on what you want to see. You will want to look out for hot spots to add to your hit list including the Space Needle, Pike Place Market and the downtown area which is always full of colorful characters. Rather than being completely free, such tours operate as 'pay what you feel tours' meaning you can give as little or as much as you are able.

Ideal for locals as well as tourists, walking tours are a great way to see all of the best parts of the city as well as the tucked away little gems that can easily be missed. It's easy to expose yourself to a world of restaurants, bars and attractions before deciding what you want to do with the rest of your trip. Walking tours come recommended to all.

Visitor Tips:

- First day in Seattle? Get used to the city in style by booking immediately.

- If you're looking to meet people the walking tours are always an all-encompassing affair; people from all over the world sign up for a true international flavor

Beneath the Streets

Opening / Closing Times – 9am-5pm

Address / Contact Number –_102 Cherry Street, Seattle, WA 98104, +1 206-624-1237

Website – http://www.beneath-the-streets.com/

Ticket Price Can you buy in advance? –$15
Average Visit Length? – 1 hour
Nearest car park (address with post code) – Impark, 98104
Nearest public transport stop –James St & 8th Avenue

Attraction Summary – To see Seattle from a completely different perspective many opt to go underground. Educational, informative and enjoyable, it's also a rather unique thing to do whilst you're in town for those who are looking for a completely different way to tackle Seattle.

The tour takes place beneath Seattle's prestigious Pioneer Square to show the history otherwise concealed by the sidewalks. With tour guides having operated in the area for many years, the experience is always incredibly informative, divulging the secrets of a bygone era. Inclusive for all, the concise nature of the tour combined with the effortless to navigate expanse makes it perfect for children as well as the elderly.

The tour then takes visitors through a plethora of tucked away tunnels tracking the cavernous passageways of five city blocks, stories central to Seattle and a thorough exploration of the architecture. Seattle is a city that can be seen in many ways including by air and see but going underground gives visitors a completely different take on the inception, design and cultivation of this stunning city. With a focus on more intimate sized groups, the tours never feel overwhelming with a firm focus on everyone in the ground keeping track of the tour guides at work.

Visitor Tips:

- If you're not one for crowds, these tours tend to be cozier and more intimate, taking less people in total

City Running Tours

Opening / Closing Times – 10am-8pm

Address / Contact Number **–** 415 Boren Ave, Seattle, WA 98104 (Downtown)/ 253-495-7297

Website – http://www.cityrunningtours.com

Ticket Price/Can you buy in advance? – Yes. Pay what you feel.
Average Visit Length? –3 hour
Nearest car park (address with post code) – 345 Boren Avenue North, 98109

Nearest public transport stop –Boren Ave and Senaca Street

Attraction Summary – Fancy seeing Seattle and keeping fit? The Seattle running tour's catchphrase is 'sweat and sightsee simultaneously' and that's exactly what it does. Runners of all levels and lifestyles pound the cities pavements including locals, tourists, travelers, marathon runners, and families, recreational and social runners.

There's an option for all making this a truly inclusive experience that's set to get your heart pounding. Completely personalized tours suit the specifications of the group taking into consideration times, longed for landmarks, routes, distance and pace. The purpose of the tours is to socialize with a variety of tours aimed at a steady casual pace that invites conservation. Highly social, this is a great way to make friends if you are new to the city.

Such tours are also ideal as a team building exercise for workers. All tours are designed with safety in mind and evade regular traffic routes to ensure that you get to see the city as you move! Sightrunning is a hugely popular attraction for running lovers which gets their hearts pumping and legs moving. Combine your love of exercise, sights and socializing as you explore this exciting city whether it's for the first time or the tenth time, you'll see the sights with fresh eyes.

Visitor Tips:

- Go alone to make new friends
- Go early in the morning for a more tranquil city experience

Seattle Cycling Tours

Opening / Closing Times – 9am-5pm

Address / Contact Number **–** 714 Pike Street, Seattle WA 98101/ +1 206-356-5803

Website – http://www.seattle-cycling-tours.com/

Ticket Price - Can you buy in advance? – Yes - $32
Average Visit Length? –3 hours
Nearest car park (address with post code) - Pike Place Market Parking - 98101
Nearest public transport stop –Pine Street

Attraction Summary – Another great sightseeing option that Seattle provides is the choice to see the city by bike. Cycling and sightseeing works well because you get to take the city in at a leisurely, casual pace that invites conservation between riders. Seattle offers spellbinding scenery, endless routes to take and very friendly locals which all contribute towards the utterly rewarding experience.

Merging exercise with socializing, by bicycle is a great way to explore the sounds and sights of the city. Occurring twice daily, it's the perfect way to meet new people. Setting off twice daily, the historical tour offers a variety of routes including downtown and Fremont to see the troll. A variety of commuters, families, large groups and individual riders take to their bicycles to see what the city has to offer.

There are day time tours and also more intense options for cycling fanatics who want to explore the city over a few days. Tour goers are also provided with a wealth of local knowledge to help the city come to life. It's also possible for riders to stop en route to sample many of the cities local cuisines whether it be a quick bakery bite or a delectable chocolate treat.

Visitor Tips:

- If you don't have your own bike you can hire one

Seattle Glassblowing Studio

Opening / Closing Times – 9am-5pm

Address / Contact Number **–** 2227 5th Ave, Seattle, WA 98121 (Downtown)/ 206-448-2181

Website – http://seattleglassblowing.com/

Ticket Price - Can you buy in advance? – Yes. $325.00
Average Visit Length? – Weekend Workshop
Nearest car park (address with post code) – Republic Parking 1420
Nearest public transport stop –5th Ave

Attraction Summary – If you're looking to learn more about glassblowing, the Seattle glassblowing studio is the ideal place to do so. Introducing guests to a highly interactive and creative experience, students can effectively learn how to make beautiful glasswork of their own.

Attendants can learn about the history of glasswork which has existed throughout ancient times, the Roman empire, the Middle Ages and the Renaissance where it eventually permeated into early American society and has remained a staple ever since. A vast array of popular glassblowing terms are introduced and explained including the blowpipe and cullet.

Created by locals, the building consists of a factory and studio where striking glassworks are created. With an option to make their own glasswork, visitors can also watch others creating beautifully striking pieces and attend an array of classes and events. Ideal for all ages, this experience is perfect for families, children, co-workers and couples who want to do something different.

There is an endless array of items to create including bowls and ornamental flowers in a variety of stunning color options for a take home treat home crafted by you. The process provides a step by step walkthrough of every aspect of glass making to help acquaint newcomers with the glittering new world of glass.

Visitor Tips:

- If you don't fancy having a go, you can just watch the professionals

The Fremont Tour

Opening / Closing Times – 9am-5pm

Address / Contact Number – Solstice Plaza, 711 N. 34th Street, Seattle, WA 98103 / +1 206-947-8112

Website –http://www.thefremonttour.com/

Ticket Price Can you buy in advance? –Yes - $20
Average Visit Length? –90 minutes
Nearest car park (address with post code) – Mercer Street Garage, 300 Mercer Street
Nearest public transport stop –Fremont Ave N & N 34th St

Summary of attraction 200 words –. Fremont is an area hot on the lists of many who opt to visit Seattle. The neighborhood itself offers a completely different side to Seattle with a welcome sign that read, 'Welcome to Fremont; Centre of the Universe.' Located over the Fremont Draw Bridge, it remains one of Seattle's most popular neighborhoods and hosts a variety of colorful characters.

With an eclectic mix of restaurants, bars, public squares and markets the entire atmosphere is playful and a little futuristic. The Fremont tour combines a standard city tour with whacky theatre and costumed guides to talk you through the cities sites.

Exploring half a mile of the suburb the tour traverses the expanse of the city and ends at a plethora of local eateries and watering holes to sate the hunger and thirst of guests. Staples of course include the Fremont Troll located beneath the bridge. It was once rumored that trolls were sighted beneath hence the erection of the marvelous photo opportunity.

Featured in many movies including '10 Things I Hate About You' people come from miles around to see the famous landmark for themselves. Incorporating props and costumes to tell the story of the city, the city's public art is brought to life in a most mesmerizing manner.

Visitor Tips:

- Feel free to dress up when you join the tour
- Make sure you take a photograph with the Fremont Troll

Emerald City Trolleys

Opening / Closing Times – 9am-5pm

Address / Contact Number –325 5th Ave N, Seattle, WA 98134 / 855-313-3456

Website –http://www.emeraldcitytrolley.com

Ticket Price - Can you buy in advance? –Yes. Varies depending on package. The hop on, hop off tour does not at present display pricing

Average Visit Length? – 1 day-3 days

Nearest car park (address with post code) **-** EMP – 401 5th Ave, Seattle 98109

Nearest public transport stop –5th Avenue

Attraction Summary – If you want to see a lot in a short time and at your own pace, Emerald City Trolley's provide a hop on hop off service that allows you to tailor your tour to your specifications. All of the city's main attractions are on offer including the Space Needle, Pike Place Market, Seattle Centre, the waterfront, downtown, The Great Wheel and Pioneers Square.

For those who want to leave the well-worn beaten track behind there is an alternate route that encapsulates Ballard, Fremont and South Lake Union. The tours are narrated by expert guides who know the city and its sights well with exquisite views on offer making this the perfect place to take your camera.

Being able to get off and on as and when you want is the perk of trip as you merge the convenience of speedy travel with your own pace and timings. You'll never feel rushed and can enjoy the city at your own pace. There are also plenty of stop offs at view points to capture the city photographically so make sure that you bring your camera with you.

The tours are also great for those with lower mobility and make the experience of seeing the city much more accessible and easy for all.

Visitor Tips:

- Plan your day so you can decide where you want to spend the most time. This will help you get the most out of your trip.

- Vehicles are open air so spring and summer are the best times to visit

Seattle's Best Restaurants

CC Image courtesy of Crystal Marie Lopez Flickr

Ellenos

Pike Place & Pike Street, Seattle, WA 98101

Ellenos real Greek yogurt is a Seattle staple. Located in the prestigious Pike Place Market, this hand crafted family recipe has become a firm favourite with locals and tourists alike. With a variety of fruits and toppings available, delectable and healthful combinations are endless and in place to tantalise every sweet tooth.

If you're in town and fancy a nutritious as well as delicious treat Ellenos offers thick, creamy and deliciously decadent options that have been voted by many as even tastier than ice cream with none of the guilty additions. It's also affordable making it the perfect portable treat as you traverse the markets.

Altura Restaurant
617 Broadway East, Seattle, WA

Located on Capitol Hill, Altura is a decadent dining experience and ideal for those that want to treat themselves to sophisticated, stylist surroundings. The gorgeous setting is ideal for couples who fancy a romantic dining experience and for those that value home grown produce bursting with flavor and healthful properties, Altura promotes only the freshest in-season foods prepared with simplicity in mind and presented prestigiously.

Eats include spicy grilled Octopus, pumpkin risotto, Neah Bay black cod, cannoli and warm chocolate budino. There's also a tasting menu presenting elegant, tongue twisting tastes that shouldn't be missed and a selection of sumptuous wines to accompany your meal.

Bakery Nouveau
4737 California Ave SW, Seattle, WA 98116-4412

Don't be put off by the queues – Bakery Nouveau has quick workers who know how to serve you speedily and are well worth waiting for. Bakery food is always quick, simple and utterly satisfying but these bakery bites are beyond beautiful. The tantalising aroma of baked bread is enough to lure you in but the plethora of available eats will leave you spoilt for choice.

People literally travel from miles around to sample the bakery's delicacies. Opt for a range of cakes, tarts and desserts available in a variety of sizes depending on whether or not you want to share, or save it all for yourself later! The flavors, aromas and presentation truly ensnare the senses and you can even have a pastry specially prepared.

Sutra

1605 N 45th St, Seattle, WA 98103-6701

Vegetarians and Vegans will absolutely adore Sutra. Organic and delicious, their range of food opens up the versatility of available herbivore centered options.

The menu is changed every two weeks meaning that you can consistently sample unique fresh produce and open up your pallet to a new array of tastes, smells, aromas, textures and ingredients. This is a great way to introduce a veggie sceptic to delicious new delicacies and also to simply revel in being a veggie with platefuls of organic, sustainable fare. Opt for seasonal squash soup or fire roasted yellow pepper. The intimate setting emboldens a sense of camaraderie and community. This is a great place to venture with a group.

Armandino's Salumi
309 Third Ave S, Seattle, WA 98104-2620

Combining an array of scrumptious cured meats, an intimate atmosphere and an array of communal dining tables, you can even help yourself to a bottle of wine at Armandino's! With an array of salami platters, porchetta and dine in and eat out options, Armandino's is a meat lover's dream.

The taste of Tuscany includes oregano salame, lamb prosciutto, pancetta, smoked paprika and lomo for a range of delicately spiced meats that blend wonderfully with the wines on offer. This is more of a lunch time joint so make sure you stop by. There's also a selection of sandwiches and pasta available for awesome on the go options.

Le Panier
1902 Pike Place, Seattle WA 98101

Conveniently located in the iconic Pike Place marketplace, Le Panier has been a Seattle institution since opening its doors in 1983. A slice of Paris in the heart of Pike, indulge in warm flaky croissants and crispy French baguettes, authentically and lovingly baked by a team of French chefs using local, seasonal ingredients.

Canlis Restaurant
2576 Aurora Ave N, Seattle, WA 98109-2206

If seafood is your vice, cocktails are your craving and wine is what you're wishing for, Canlis is a superb place to stop in at. The fine dining experience offers diners phenomenal views of Seattle's skyline in an intimate and yet elite way.

The soft glow lighting creates a decadent atmosphere ideal for couples and large celebratory parties. Be aware this is a dinner only joint. Established in 1950, Canlis offers strikingly gorgeous options such as steak tartare, oysters, pork collar, swordfish, sea bass, wagyu and delectable additions including truffle fries and forest mushrooms. Dessert is to die for with sorbet and chocolate fondants aplenty.

Pike Place Chowder
1530 Post Alley, Seattle, WA 98101

Pike Place is the place to be with its heaving markets, endless stream of meandering market goers and eccentric oddities. If you're in town and hungry, escape the hustle and bustle with a steaming bowl of flavorful chowder.

Piping hot must haves include the market chowder and New England clam chowder. You can opt to eat in or take your chowder with you as you explore this most historical market. There's also a happy hour which is perfect if you want to save a little money as you tuck into these most edible of eats. Warm yourself on a winter's day with a scrumptious bowl of chowder.

Tat's Deli
159 Yesler Way, Seattle, WA 98104

Seattle has borrowed a little NY cool with this tucked away treasure. Mouthwatering and delicious, this little hot spot offers up generous platefuls of soups, salads and sides but its most famous for its heaving hot subs and specials.

There's also a range of Philly Steaks and Hoagies and ice cool beverages to wash it all down with. Opt for the meatball, hot turkey or hot pastrami sub for delicious meat mouthfuls. The crispy chicken sub and chicken bacon ranch also come highly recommended. If you're extra hungry, opt for a twinburger sub. This delicious little deli is perfect for the hungry wanderer. Add hot chips for a real winner.

Fran's Chocolates
1325 1st Ave, Seattle, WA 98101

If you feel like indulging your sweet tooth, head to Fran's chocolates. Tantalizing temptations include truffles, caramels, fruit and nuts and whole bars. Each little bite is beautifully adorned and oozes a delirium inducing filling that will have you coming back again and again.

Salted caramels, dark chocolate truffles and gold bars and gold bites make sumptuous little snacks to die for. You can also purchase gift boxes for your loved ones including creamy white chocolate coconut bars. Like a mini Willy Wonka's chocolate factory, Fran's chocolates are famous and make the perfect decadent treat when you're in town.

Travelling Around Seattle

Seattle is a city that has to be seen and that means researching your travel options.

1. **Walking**

   For the most part, Seattle is a very walkable city. A lot of landmarks are within close capacity of one another meaning that you can see a vast array of attractions within close proximity.

2. **Bus**

   Seattle is well connected with an extensive and easy to follow bus system. You can easily see all of the main attractions by bus using the trip planner or Google maps options to plan your route.

   There are four particular transits in central Seattle; King Country Metro, Community Transit, Pierce Transit and Sound Transit. The bus is also a great way to rub shoulders with the locals and the colorful characters of the city. You can ride bus 99 into Chinatown or up to Pioneer Square. Broad Street is the stop for the Space Needle. The two key bus services in Seattle are King Country Metro and Sound Transit.

   Sound Transit covers longer distances and is designed more so with commuters in mind and the Metro bus focuses on the city center itself.

3. Link Light Rail

The Link Light Rail connects the Seatac International Airport with Westlake Station with a total of 11 stops in between. It's a highly cost-effective option, particularly if you are travelling alone.

Trains run frequently, approximately every 7, 10 and 15 minutes, so there's always another train on the way if you miss the first. The Tacoma Link light Rail takes you to downtown Tacoma in only 5 stops and runs every 12 to 24 minutes. The best thing about the Tacoma line is that it is completely free.

4. Monorail

The monorail is pretty historic and also a great way to get around. Jump on at downtown Seattle which takes you to Seattle center directly to the Space Needle and nearby attractions. There are departures every 10 minutes daily. The mile trip is covered in only 2 minutes.

5. The Seattle Streetcar

Jump on at the Southlake Union line to take the 2.6 trip that takes you from Westlake Centre to the South Lake Union area.

6. Sound Transit

Taking you between Tacoma and Seattle, this service runs weekday mornings and evenings only.

7. Washington State Ferries

When in Washington you simply have to experience a ferry ride. You can travel to many of the off-shore islands from Seattle and go on many a day trip.

8. Water Taxi

The King County water taxi service ferries passengers between West Seattle and Vashon Island from Downtown. They leave from pier 50 south of the State ferry dock.

9. ORCA card

If you're in Seattle for a while, you'll want to invest in an ORCA card. Named after the whales that breach the waters nearby, ORCA cards are accepted on all forms of public transport and can be purchased for $5 and loaded with cash.

What's On

Because events are added and changed all the time it would be impossible for a guide book to feature them all accurately.

Below are some valuable websites that help ensure you see the events you want.

Events month by month
http://www.events12.com/seattle/

Shows and Concerts
http://www.seattle-theatre.com/index_concert.php

Convention Center
http://www.scaaevent.org/

Key Arena
http://www.keyarena.com/events

Baseball – Seattle Mariners
http://seattle.mariners.mlb.com

Football – Seahawks
http://www.seahawks.com/

Ice Hockey – Thunderbirds
http://www.seattlethunderbirds.com/

Made in the USA
San Bernardino, CA
08 November 2015